# Hellfires of Grief II:
# More
# Love Poems

*C. Eldon Taylor*

# Hellfires of Grief II: More Love Poems

©2014 C. Eldon Taylor

All rights reserved. No part of this book may be reproduced in any form or by any means, electronic or mechanical, including photocopying, recording, or by any information storage and retrieval system, without written permission except in the case of brief quotations embodied in critical articles and reviews.

ISBN: 0692314121
ISBN-13: 978-0692314128

LCCN: 2014918687

Printed in USA
by CreateSpace
an Amazon.com Company

Published by
C. Eldon Taylor
Henrico, Virginia 23228

# Introduction

**Hellfires of Grief: Love Poems** (Hellfires I) is a collection of 222 poems written during the first eighteen months of my bereavement following the disembodiment of my beloved Carol Susan. **Hellfires of Grief II: More Love Poems** (Hellfires II) is a collection of 222 poems written during the second eighteen months of my bereavement. Together **Hellfires I** and **Hellfires II** cover the first three years of my experiences of loss, grief, despair, and the slow transformation from seeing only with eyes of loss to also seeing with eyes of love. The combined 444 poems provide an intense and intimate look at my journey into the hellfires of grief and black nights of the soul after the disembodiment of my soulmate. The companion to **Hellfires I**, **Golden Dreams I** presents 111 dreams converted into poems covering the same time period as **Hellfires I**. Golden dreams provide the healing energy of the spirit realm. **Golden Dreams II**, currently in process, covers the time period of **Hellfires II** and beyond. The 444 Hellfires poems summarize my waking daytime experiences while the 222 Golden Dream poems summarize my dreaming nighttime experiences. The poems provide a glimpse of the healing energy of the spirit realm which has facilitated my transformation from seeing only from eyes of loss into also seeing from eyes of love.

While the transformation is a life's journey, I am sharing the first three years of my bereavement experience with the intent to offer assistance to others experiencing their own hellfires of grief. In a culture where dying, death, and grief are taboo, my decision to share my experiences of the first three years of my bereavement is an attempt to offer alternatives to the conventional wisdom of just getting on with one's life. Grieving and bereavement honor and venerate disembodied love ones maintaining a flowing of healing energies between the beings of spirit and embodied souls.

As one of the poems (*poems & POEMS,* page 122) states, my poems are not POEMS nor POETRY nor ART nor am I a POET. I am a wounded human being licking my woundedness with words. It is my hope, wish, and intent that sharing the words I use to lick my woundedness after the loss of my beloved will offer a measure of comfort and healing energy. May the words lick your woundedness and assist your healing transformation. May you be blessed seeing from eyes of love. May you and yours be blessed with golden dreams and eternal love.

C. Eldon Taylor<br>
October 31, 2014

# Hellfires of Grief II: More Love Poems

## Table of Contents

### 1977                                                   Page

| | |
|---|---|
| Carol Susan     March 27, 1977 | 1 |

### 2013

| | |
|---|---|
| CS Birthday 2013: May 8 | 2 |
| Tale of the Elephant: May 8 | 4 |
| Chrysalis of Grief: May 9 | 9 |
| Three Monkeys to Four: May 9 | 10 |
| Orchid Weeping: May 13 | 11 |
| Mothering Ones Day 2013: May 12 | 13 |
| Life's Sweetness: May 13 | 14 |
| Separate Realities: May 15 | 16 |
| More Than You Know: May 19 | 19 |
| Background Foreground: May 19 | 20 |
| Eyes of Love Eyes of Loss II: May 22 | 23 |
| Abstracting Experience: May 22 | 24 |
| Wounded Healer: May 26 | 26 |
| 1-800-Bad Drug: May 31 | 28 |
| Triple Vision: May 31 | 29 |
| First Book: June 4 | 30 |
| Missing My Kitten II: June 10 | 31 |
| Golden Hands: June 13 | 32 |
| Not My Time: June 21 | 33 |
| Too Many Moves: June 19 | 34 |
| Six Hundred Days: June 25 | 38 |
| Indispensible: June 30 | 40 |
| Tip of Iceberg: July 1 | 42 |

| | |
|---|---|
| Well Meaning Advice: July 1 | 43 |
| Kitten's Nine Lives: July 4 | 44 |
| Two Realms: July 5 | 46 |
| Maya's Guardian: July 7 | 48 |
| Crispbread Crackers: July 7 | 50 |
| Boars Hair Brush: July 8 | 52 |
| Grandmother Spider's Compassion: July 17 | 54 |
| Most Beautiful Flowers: July 26 | 56 |
| Days of Observance: July 29 | 58 |
| 35$^{th}$ Wedding Anniversary: July 30 | 61 |
| Celestial Dream Catcher: August 1 | 62 |
| Dream Catcher Revelation: August 1 | 64 |
| Grief and Four Elements: August 11 | 66 |
| I Miss You: August 10 | 68 |
| Not Real Too Real: August 11 | 69 |
| Two Realms II: August 11 | 70 |
| Double Simian Crease: August 13 | 72 |
| My Path and I Ching II: August 16 | 73 |
| Withered Up II: August 16 | 74 |
| Luck: August 16 | 78 |
| My Birthday 2013: August 20 | 80 |
| Golden Hands II: August 23 | 82 |
| Grow Old With Me II: August 26 | 84 |
| Twenty Two Months: August 31 | 86 |
| Chakra Cleaning: August 31 | 88 |
| Question Why: September 6 | 90 |
| Hurricane Winds: September 8 | 94 |
| Loving Acts of Kindness: September 9 | 95 |
| Self Indulgent: September 12 | 96 |
| Blessed With Golden Dreams: Sept 14 | 98 |
| Found Again: September 15 | 99 |
| Wedding Rings: September 15 | 100 |
| Quest Painting: September 15 | 102 |
| Amplification: September 15 | 103 |
| Halloween: September 17 | 104 |

| | |
|---|---|
| Dance Floor of Time: September 22 | 106 |
| Miss You Today: September 26 | 107 |
| New Hero Myth: September 23 | 108 |
| Seven Hundred Days: September 30 | 110 |
| Watching: October 1 | 113 |
| Angels of Mercy: October 1 | 114 |
| Making Patacones: October 6 | 116 |
| Despair: October 6 | 117 |
| Red Leaf at Your Shrine: October 6 | 118 |
| Contamination: October 6 | 120 |
| poems & POEMS: October 9 | 122 |
| Not Here Today: October 9 | 123 |
| Thousand Years: October 10 | 124 |
| Dish Drain Board: October 20 | 126 |
| Small Clothes: October 23 | 127 |
| Dream Vision: October 27 | 129 |
| Black Lightning: October 28 | 130 |
| Disembodiment Day: Year Two: Oct 31 | 132 |
| Last Five Years: Oct 31 | 137 |
| Accidentally On Purpose: Oct 31 | 138 |
| Monkfish: November 1 | 140 |
| Day and Night: November 5 | 142 |
| Second Book: November 11 | 144 |
| Healing Poems: November 13 | 147 |
| Counting My Blessings: November 15 | 148 |
| No Contest: November 16 | 150 |
| Fireplace in Chester: November 21 | 152 |
| Cats Playing: November 22 | 154 |
| Thanksgiving Three: November 24 | 157 |
| Black Thanksgivings: November 25 | 158 |
| Spoiled Rotten: November 26 | 160 |
| School of Grief: November 26 | 163 |
| All Golden Dreams: December 1 | 164 |
| Sometimes: December 4 | 166 |
| Few Minutes Into Forever: Dec 5 | 167 |

| | |
|---|---|
| Sneaking Up On Paradox: Dec 8 | 168 |
| Looking at Memories: Dec 9 | 170 |
| Changing Forms: Dec 12 | 171 |
| Advisor to Companion: Dec 19 | 172 |
| Dragon Named Grief: Dec 19 | 174 |
| Sharing Winter Solstices: Dec 21 | 176 |
| New Way of Sharing: Dec 22 | 180 |
| Christmas 2013: Dec 25 | 182 |
| Forgotten Golden Dreams: Dec 26 | 185 |
| Careful Wishing: Dec 31 | 186 |

**2014**

| | |
|---|---|
| New Years 2014: Jan 1 | 188 |
| Fortune Cookies: Jan 1 | 190 |
| Spirit Realm Resident: Jan 2 | 191 |
| Superior Attitude & I Ching: Jan 4 | 192 |
| Enduring Relationship: Jan 5 | 193 |
| Lake of Longing: Jan 8 | 194 |
| Eight Hundred Days: Jan 9 | 195 |
| Possession Beyond Measure: Jan 13 | 198 |
| Struggling: Jan 13 | 199 |
| Alchemy of Grief: Jan 20 | 200 |
| Embodied Companions: Jan 20 | 202 |
| Ultimate Rescue: Jan 21 | 204 |
| Lauren's Procedure: Jan 24 | 206 |
| Enough Not Enough: Jan 24 | 207 |
| Lunar New Year Cards 2014: Jan 24 | 209 |
| Honoring the Dead: Jan 26 | 210 |
| Heart of Grief: Jan 29 | 212 |
| Lunar New Year 2014: Jan 31 | 214 |
| "the dead": Jan 31 | 216 |
| Transcending Dual Realms: Feb 2 | 218 |
| Well of Dreams: Feb 3 | 220 |
| Restoration Miracle: Feb 6 | 222 |
| Lost Puppy: Feb 9 | 224 |
| Black Water: Feb 10 | 225 |

| | |
|---|---|
| Valentine's Day 2014: Feb 14 | 226 |
| Balance: Feb 24 | 227 |
| Balance II: Feb 25 | 230 |
| Horrible Present: Feb 26 | 231 |
| Twenty Eight Months: Feb 28 | 232 |
| Spirals of Grief: March 1 | 234 |
| Pretending: March 4 | 236 |
| Never Expected: March 6 | 237 |
| DeVaney-Wong Workbook: March 9 | 238 |
| Three Four: March 9 | 240 |
| Lightning of Love: March 11 | 241 |
| Making Room: March 13 | 242 |
| Doubly Blessed: March 14 | 244 |
| Sharing Quintessence: March 17 | 245 |
| Miniature Distillery: March 17 | 246 |
| Alchemy of Longing Love Loss: March 18 | 248 |
| Domain Names: March 22 | 250 |
| Ugly Grief Demon: March 22 | 251 |
| Eggs In One Basket: March 22 | 252 |
| Easy Decision: March 23 | 253 |
| All Better: March 25 | 255 |
| Curling Up: March 30 | 256 |
| Greed: March 31 | 258 |
| Dreamtime Comfort: April 4 | 260 |
| 888: April 8 | 261 |
| Salsa: April 10 | 262 |
| Naming Things: April 10 | 263 |
| Seasons of Grief: April 10 | 264 |
| A Love Eternal: April 12 | 266 |
| Over and Over: April 12 | 267 |
| Dreaming: April 13 | 268 |
| False Mastery: April 13 | 269 |
| Transformation: April 16 | 270 |
| Alchemy of the Heart: April 19 | 272 |
| Easter 2014: April 20 | 273 |

| | |
|---|---|
| 900 Days: April 20 | 274 |
| I Remember: April 22 | 275 |
| Black Lead of Grief: April 26 | 276 |
| Half A Heart: April 28 | 277 |
| Some Days: April 29 | 278 |
| Embodied Companion: April 29 | 279 |
| Photographs: April 29 | 280 |
| Thirty Months: April 30 | 281 |
| All My Heart: May 1 | 284 |
| Soror Mystica: May 1 | 285 |
| Pregnant With Death: May 7 | 287 |
| Carol Susan's Birthday: May 8 | 288 |
| Mothers Day 2014: May 11 | 291 |
| Return: June 1 | 292 |
| Cottage's Energy: June 12 | 294 |
| True Shrine: June 17 | 296 |
| Invisible: June 30 | 297 |
| Empty Nest: June 30 | 298 |
| Despair II: July 1 | 300 |
| A Few Moments: July 17 | 304 |
| Dreams Underground: July 23 | 305 |
| 999: July 29 | 307 |
| 1000 and 36: July 30 | 308 |
| Blessed: August 5 | 310 |
| Alone II: August 6 | 311 |
| Disbelief: August 6 | 312 |
| Projects: August 6 | 315 |
| Wolves of Despair: August 9 | 316 |
| Pink Disposable Razors: August 9 | 318 |
| Pink Disposable Razors II: August 9 | 319 |
| NO!: August 10 | 320 |
| WHY?: August 10 | 321 |
| DAMN!: August 10 | 322 |
| NO! WHY? DAMN!: August 11 | 323 |
| Tai Chi Flag: August 13 | 325 |

| | |
|---|---|
| Sharing Lychees: August 14 | 326 |
| Beach Condo 1977: August 19 | 327 |
| Beach Condo Recreated: August 19 | 328 |
| Dirty Navel: August 19 | 329 |
| My Birthday 2014: August 20 | 330 |
| Inadequate Words: August 22 | 331 |
| Mysteries: August 25 | 332 |
| Dreaming II: September 3 | 333 |
| Things: September 8 | 334 |
| Presences: September 8 | 335 |
| Sadness Attacks: September 13 | 336 |
| Halloween 1977: September 14 | 337 |
| Eternal Love: September 15 | 338 |
| Simple Pleasures: September 15 | 339 |
| Physical Touch: September 15 | 341 |
| Heavy Heart: September 22 | 342 |
| Poquito Energy: October 8 | 344 |
| Looking Back: October 13 | 346 |
| Black Year Four: October 17 | 348 |
| Healing Energy: October 19 | 349 |
| Laboratory of Alchemy: October 19 | 350 |
| Disembodiment Day Year Three: Oct 31 | 352 |
| Hellfires of Grief III: October 31 | 356 |
| **Carol Susan    March 27, 2014** | **361** |
| Acknowledgements | 362 |
| Selected References | 363 |
| Author | 367 |
| Other Books | 369 |

*Carol Susan*

# Carol Susan

numinous power of the Feminine

natural expression of mysterious Yin ways

primal archetypal image of Woman

essence of flowering lotus

enchanting mythological princess

beautiful daughter of Tara

transformation's Divine Vessel

from you I see my changing

you guide by being you


you are also changing


we are becoming friends

C. Eldon Taylor<br>March 27, 1977

# Carol Susan's Birthday 2013

if embodied you would be fifty nine
second birthday we observed
since you disembodied
your birthdays were
happy celebrations
now we miss your physical being
most intensely on your birthday

this year I gave you two presents
collection of 222 poems
Hellfires of Grief: Love Poems
put the original copy
on your shrine
to be replaced with
final printed version
made dual soul dream catcher
for your second present
perhaps more for me than you
gold web purple frame
catches celestial dreams
left side spirit realm
right side physical realm
overlapping space
threshold portal doorway
between two realms
with Grandmother Spider
at the center
web belongs to Her
made two rainbow bodies

from stone beads
for spirit realm side
made only one for physical realm side
you ask what happened to yours
added second rainbow body
to physical realm side
placed dual soul dream catcher
over your picture at your shrine

we ate Chinese food
quiet day sad day
you would be fifty-nine
if embodied
age is irrelevant in spirit realm
you appear in golden dreams
radiant golden rainbow goddess
golden rainbow angel
golden rainbow dragon
radiant golden celestial being
words cannot properly describe

we observed your birthday
gave you presents
ate your favorite food
know you like your presents
now your birthdays make me sad
making the best of it
easier said than done
sometimes making the best of it
is just holding on
hoping dual soul dream catcher
catches celestial golden dreams

May 8, 2013

# Tale of the Elephant and Visually Impaired Retold

in earlier tale
group of visually impaired
individuals trying to
describe nature
of an elephant
each individual holding
a different part
so nature of
an elephant
dependent upon
part the individual
touches
so reality depends on
part you are holding

in new tale two traditions
describing the nature of the
elephant
religion and science

religion determines
elephant's gray color
indicates sin as if elephant
without sin would be white
pure without sin
so religion proceeds to wash
elephant with ever stronger cleaners
but elephant does not turn white

rather turns red
bleeding to death
from overly aggressive cleaning
purification efforts
religion then states
at least elephant's soul free
released from sinful body
no other way
to redeem elephant

science thinks religion's description
of elephant's gray skin
indicating sin
superstition
utter folly
science proceeds to describe
elephant in exhaustive detail
with extreme precision
every measurement possible
of elephant's external anatomy
science determines more studies
needed to determine how
elephant functions
science speculates there are
parts of elephant
hidden from view
internal
that explains how
elephant functions
since surface studies
proved inconclusive
science determines few minor
procedures indicated
to determine how elephant functions

so dissects elephant
during procedures
elephant dies
science continues to dissect
elephant into ever smaller units
frisky elephant transformed
into frisky dirt
then microscopic dirt
no longer frisky
subatomic dirt
science eventually pronounces
elephants not fit subjects
for scientific study
as they stop functioning
after few minor procedures
in conclusion science
determines elephants
much too fragile
to be viable species
science wonders how
elephants managed to survive
science pronounces
elephants destined
for extinction
since they have such
fragile constitutions
nor could they be of any
real value as they stop
functioning after only
few minor scientific procedures

elephant was much better off
when group of visually impaired
individuals were standing around

each holding
one of elephant's external body parts

we are all visually impaired
each in their own way
religion and science
have turned their respective
visual impairments into
industries
institutions
instructing people how to see
with their respective
version of visual impairment
denial and mystification
of visual experience
you did not see anything
there was nothing to see
not real
only your imagination
lights playing tricks
fatigue
blood sugar
electrolyte imbalance
temptations of the devil

we all suffer from visual impairment
one way or another
even those of us without
physical problems with their eyes
many receive instructions from
both institutions
resulting in
double visual impairment

if elephants were wise
would stay as far away
from religion and science
as possible
might then be fortunate
to live into old age
experience a life of simple pleasures
free from restraints of religion
reductionism of science
nature does not need to
submit to either one

May 8, 2013

# Chrysalis of Grief

at first grief dragon
dark heavy black worm
raw with grief
over time worm
spins cocoon
spinning itself inside
leaking oozing grief
cocoon transforms
slowly
luminous chrysalis
containing golden rainbow dragon
beautiful celestial being
so I have been told
few glimpses
golden rainbow aura
still in chrysalis of grief
black worm
remembers
golden rainbow dragon
visit in golden dreams
other experiences

May 9, 2013

# Three Monkeys to Four

hear no evil
see no evil
speak no evil
three monkeys
hands over ears
hands over eyes
hands over mouth
three monkeys

fourth monkey
do no evil
hands over crotch
fourth monkey
slow progress

what will fifth monkey
be covering
fifth monkey
waiting for more people to
pay attention
to first four
slow progress

perhaps fifth monkey
will be covering its heart
feel no evil
hands over heart
not yet available in stores
slow progress

May 9, 2013

# Orchid Weeping

looking at tidied up shrine
old clutter comforting
more difficult
letting go of past
than putting items in a box

purple orchid
got for your shrine
for Valentine's Day
losing its blooms
flowers started dropping off
before eighteen months
observance of your disembodiment
more fell before
your birthday
mothers day
mothering ones day
orchid weeping
reflection of my own
sad times
orchid weeping
with me

May 13, 2013

# Mothering Ones Day 2013

missing your physical being
mothering ones day
second since you disembodied
you became my mothering one long ago
I became yours
we mothered each other
wonderful experiences
wonderful memories
my physical mothering one
thirty-four years
now my spirit mothering one
golden hands holding
my broken hearts together
golden energy helping me heal
shared golden dreams
golden rainbow embraces
wonderful experiences
wonderful memories
blessed with my
embodied mothering one
blessed beyond measure
with my spirit mothering one
thank you for being
my mothering one
send you all my love
essence of mothering
happy mothering ones day
my spirit mothering one

May 12, 2013

# Life's Sweetness

life's sweetness started changing
with your symptoms
becoming bitter sour
with your diagnosis
some sweetness returned
after your recovery from surgery
for a while
reoccurrence
bitter sour returned
sweetness left when
you disembodied
life's sweetness gone
replaced with grief
raw heavy black grief
hellfires of grief
dark nights of the soul

you brought life's sweetness
when we met
life's sweetness left with you
you have always been
my life's sweetness
now I have sweet memories
of our life together

I am suppose to be making
the best of it
sometimes more difficult
than others
eighteen months
your birthday

mother's day
mothering ones day
all in a row
looking back at
life's sweet memories
with eyes of loss
making the best of it
easier said than done

life's sweetness
returns in golden dreams
thankful I remember a few
wish I could remember them all
life's sweetness
golden dreams
shared with you
sweet memories
life's sweetness
shared with you
very appreciative
you brought
life's sweetness
very appreciative
you still do

May 13, 2013

# Separate Realities

physical realm - spirit realm
separate realities
ordinary reality - nonordinary reality
separate realities
seen world - unseen world
separate realities

some visit spirit realm awake
altered consciousness
visions journeys
everyone visits spirit realm
in dreams
some even remember
I remember golden dreams
shared with my beloved
golden dream visits to spirit realm

spirit realm superior to physical realm
remember spirit realm visits in
golden dreams
when awake in physical realm
do not remember physical realm
in golden dreams

spirit realm has many names
heaven paradise nirvana
to name only a few
celestial realm
golden radiant energy
light and love

physical world has many names too
mixed realm
where dualism polarities exist
love loss
love hate
peace war
joy pain
hunger plenty
scoop or two of heaven
mixed with equal measures of hell
stirred with chaos
heated in hellfires of grief
leavened with dark nights of the soul

since black times started
prefer spirit realm visits
golden dreams
to physical realm
always disappointed to wake up
not remember
dream time visits to spirit realm
golden dreams
treasure the ones I remember
reread them now and then

know separate realities
love - loss of physical realm
golden love of spirit realm
blessed with golden dreams
shared with my beloved
visits to spirit realm

May 15, 2013

# More Than You Know

Carol Susan used to tell me
"I love you more than
you will ever know"
I did not fully understand
then
I have much better idea
now
Carol Susan's golden love
reaching out from spirit realm
crossing the veil
which for her does not exist
embracing me with golden love
healing my broken hearts with
golden hands
providing me with messages
inspirations
sharing wonderful golden dreams
her golden rainbow spirit
illuminating our shared
golden cocoon

Carol Susan used to tell me
"I love you more than
you will ever know"
I have much better idea
now

May 19, 2013

# Background Foreground

at first grief all consuming
dominating psychic landscape
nothing else mattered
with one exception
grieving loss of my soulmate
everything else faded away
everything else insignificant
with one exception
ate a little slept a little
cried a lot
everything reminded me of loss
largest part of foreground
part no longer there
embodied beloved disembodied
missing physical being
took up all the space
all the space in my mind
all the space in my heart
all the space in my world
nothing else mattered
with one exception
only focus loss missing grief
heartache longing despair
hellfires of grief
dark nights of the soul

at first did not recognize
my efforts to survive
form of healing
enduring loss grief heartache
heartbreak longing despair
landscape black ugly
grieving all consuming

nothing else mattered
with one exception
established ceremonies
burned incense all day
most of the night
slept a little
cried a lot
established my beloved's shrine
sacred space
sanctuary to grieve
feel closer to my beloved
started writing in our journal
daily love letters to my beloved
knew at some level
my efforts a form of healing
disembodiment of my beloved
broke my hearts open wide
heart of my hearts
moved from background
to foreground
better able to hear
soft whispers of
heart of my hearts
horrible way to access
improve intuition
spirit vision

heart of my hearts
knew my beloved not gone
only changed forms
physical being to
subtle spirit being
celestial being
golden rainbow angel
started to wonder when
my beloved would appear

in my dreams
wrote in our journal
hoping wishing asking
for my beloved to appear
signs messages
wanted needed
desperately needed
dream visit from my beloved

golden dream
first of many
blessed with golden dreams
at first did not fully appreciate
healing power of golden dreams
spirit realm visits with my beloved
golden dreams
healing energy of love
shared foreground with loss grief
grief dragon overwhelmed by
golden dreams
moving towards more balance
between loss grief and golden dreams
loss still foreground
now shared with golden dreams
energy of love
moving slowly towards balance
blessed by golden dreams
healing spirit realm visits
with my beloved

May 21, 2013

# Eyes of Love Eyes of Loss II

at first eyes of loss prevailed
eyes of love over whelmed by loss
eyes of loss   grief vision
eyes of love   spirit vision
many months two ways of seeing
switched back and forth
expected would always be
one or the other
golden dreams strengthening
eyes of love   spirit vision
weakening eyes of loss   grief vision
then moment when
vision changed
clear mixture of two ways of seeing
combined coexisting
simultaneous
double vision
as if evenly matched
small still point in middle
still too small to enter
large enough to experience
another level of healing
new eyes fresh eyes
double vision
blessed to have new way of seeing
new eyes
fresh eyes
another level of healing

May 22, 2013

Note: *Eyes of Love Eyes of Loss*, **Hellfires I**, December 6, 2012, page 152

# Abstracting Experience

learning language
abstracting experience into words
form of wounding
describing experience
labeling experience
one step removed
from direct experience
with each level of abstraction
another step removed
ever more precise abstraction
more and more
removed from experience
each step removed
another level of wounding

flying things first level
birds second
owls become snowy white owls
young old male female
flying roosting
stuffed in a museum
manufactured toy
on and on
abstracting experience
form of wounding

learning language necessary skill
not necessary to understand language
as way of abstracting experience
as way of wounding
learning to read abstract marks
write abstract marks
necessary skills

not necessary to understand language
as form of abstracting experience
as form of wounding

you may not believe
abstracting experience
form of wounding
no blame
you may not believe
understanding about
abstracting experience
as form of wounding
necessary for healing
or that not healing
from abstracting
has a cost
no blame
I am hoping to experience
snowy white owl directly
others too
different kind of healing
not necessary for everyone
no blame
disconnecting from
abstracting experience to
experiencing world as a child
relearning direct experience
oneness rather than duality
unity rather than separateness
requires unlearning to have
direct experience
superior healing

May 22, 2013

# Wounded Healer

been said wounded healer heals best
may be true
only if wounded healer
first heals themselves
often easier said than done
easy to write story of being
wounded healer
victim
unable to move beyond
victim wounded story
envision healing
letting go of victim role
security of known misery

been said wounded healer heals best
not true if wound's
still raw
hemorrhaging energy
when my beloved disembodied
my wound almost fatal
holding on by a thread
wounded victim
unable to see beyond my woundedness
did not consider healing
barely holding on
unable to conceive healing myself
much less others
presumptuous to even consider
healing others
inflict my woundedness on others
needed psychic first aid myself

others have to wait
barely able to endure my own wound
almost fatal
holding on by a thread
hearts broken in two
hellfires of grief
dark nights of the soul
grieving hemorrhaging energy
despair almost fatal wound
abundance of compassion
little energy for healing others
with few exceptions
little energy for healing myself
did not consider healing at first

started to receive healing energy
golden dreams shared with my beloved
golden dreams healing energy
started to become aware
golden dreams
transformative
healing process
staunching hemorrhaging
healing journey
recovering energy lost with
my beloved's disembodiment

been said wounded healer heals best
may be true
still too early in my healing journey
to know

                                      May 26, 2013

# 1 800 Bad Drug

rarely watch television
once or twice a month
taking a break
watching 30 minutes
advertisement for
1 800 Bad Drug
looked it up online
awful news
weeks later
watching election returns
advertisement for
1 800 Bad Drug
awful news
potential side effects
include
pancreatic cancer
death
my beloved took the drug
two and a half years
may answer why
my beloved disembodied
prematurely
expedited
by a bad drug
does not change my loss
provides focus for my anger
life prematurely abbreviated
by a bad drug
awful news

May 31, 2013
Nineteen Months

# Triple Vision

beyond eyes of loss   eyes of love
grief vision   spirit vision
beyond two ways of seeing
combined grief vision spirit vision
third way of seeing
vision across realms
physical realm   spirit realm
coexisting
embodied soul vision
access to both ways of seeing
no longer separate ways of seeing
double vision becomes triple vision
third way of seeing
or
all ways of seeing
combined
superior vision
have had glimpses
golden dreams
superior way of seeing
embodied soul vision
another level of healing
superior way of seeing
soul vision

May 31, 2013
Nineteen Months

# First Book

large quantity of our first book came today
not book I had ever thought of writing
not book I had ever envisioned writing
unfortunately book I had to write
at least I had to write poems
soul's need heart of my hearts' need
had to publish poems too
give something back help others
intense book painful book
painful experiences painful reality
put books under your shrine
put first one on your shrine
wrote
*number one*
*to Carol Susan*
*I love you always forever and beyond*
*your little Carlos Eldon*
made me cry

setting here wondering
how many books would it take
to be enough
not enough trees
not
enough
trees
nowhere near enough

June 4, 2013

# Missing My Kitten II

eighty-four weeks
missing my kitten
embodied kitten
shared physical realm life
spoiled by your love

now celestial kitten
spoiled by my celestial kitten
wonderful golden rainbow love
wonderful yet not the same
eighty-four weeks
missing my kitten
embodied kitten
no point counting
heart of my hearts knows
will always
miss my kitten

very intense missing
heart of my hearts missing
embodied soul missing
missing my kitten
embodied kitten
eighty-four weeks
no point counting
heart of my hearts knows
will always
miss my kitten

June 10, 2013

Note: *Missing My Kitten*, **Hellfires I**, January 7, 2013, page 196

# Golden Hands

your golden hands
holding my broken hearts together
helping me heal
I am holding them together too
working to heal my broken hearts
sometimes my small self does not care
healing too much work
stay broken bleeding

I like knowing your golden hands
hold my broken hearts together
healing with your golden love
you have always held my hearts
in your golden hands
always forever and beyond
my golden hands and yours
holding our hearts together
always forever and beyond
spoiled by your loving touch
golden hands holding my hearts
powerful golden healing
transcends my small self
golden hands holding
my broken hearts together
blessed by the healing touch
of your golden hands
holding my broken hearts together
thank you for your loving touch

June 13, 2013

# Not My Time

when you disembodied
I wanted to come along
part of me did
at least half of my heart
perhaps more
a lot more
holding on by a thread
not my time
I wanted to come along
not my time
seems I still have work to do
lessons to learn
not my time
hope lessons not about recovery
healing difficult enough
ongoing process
never fully healed
still do not know
what healing looks like
much less recovery
only know it is
not my time
know what healing looks like
know what recovery looks like too
not my time
still have work to do
lessons to learn
not my time

June 21, 2013

# Too Many Moves

started beach front Indialantic Florida
first six months together
moved to opposite side of A1A
Indialantic Florida
moved to Richmond Virginia
moved to Chester Virginia
moved to Colonial Heights Virginia
our daughter born first house there
moved to larger house in
Colonial Heights Virginia
new job
moved to Jeffersonton Virginia
then to Warrenton Virginia
you loved the little town
our house three blocks from
center of town
new job
moved to Potomac Maryland
two houses there
new job
moved to Weston Florida
then larger house Hollywood Florida
twelve years
new job
I moved to Tampa Florida
you were to follow
you became ill
temporary move to Baltimore Maryland
Johns Hopkins whipple surgery
back to Hollywood Florida
moved to Henrico Virginia

little cottage we fixed up
picked things out together
lived in our little cottage
little over a year
early October 2010 to
October 31, 2011
you disembodied
later thinking about our last move
realized you moved us
to Richmond area
knew you were going to die
disembody soon
you thought I would do better
living in Richmond area
third time

now in our little cottage
where you disembodied
realized you knew
you were going to die
disembody
taking care of your beloved
as best as you could
loving act makes me cry
took several months
after your disembodiment
for me to realize
your plan
massive denial
looking for a miracle

thinking about too many moves
moved to Iowa City Iowa
mutual support our daughter and me

since you disembodied
moved again Coralville Iowa
so many moves
last two without you
in your physical body
you moved too of course
your spirit always comes along
first at our cottage
then to Iowa City
now to Coralville
moving did not used to make me cry
now moving makes me cry
packing up your shrine
remembering too many moves
picking out our little cottage
where you came to die
now moving makes me cry
too many moves
I visit our little cottage
looks much like it did
after we fixed it up
one difference
awful difference
your physical person gone
disembodied
your ashes in your urn
all that remains of
your physical person
your ashes move with us
more important
you spirit does too
now each move makes me cry
remembering
too many moves

took several months
after your disembodiment
for me to realize
we moved to Richmond area
as you knew you were going to die
disembody
taking care of your beloved
as best as you could
loving act still makes me cry
have I done any better
in Richmond area
perhaps
but not by much
losing the physical person
of my soulmate
worst experience of my life
little cottage we picked our together
fixed up together
offers some comfort
we talked about having a little cottage
for years
did not expect we would select
our little cottage where you would die
disembody so soon
leaving me without your physical person
in our little cottage
makes me cry
so many moves
too many moves
now moving makes me cry

June 19, 2013

# Six Hundred Days

six hundred days
since you disembodied
your beautiful radiant spirit
returned to our spirit realm home
today wondered how
many times my hearts can break
until pieces are microscopic
wondered if that is what
healing looks like
pieces too small to see
know not correct
pieces reform over and over
your golden hands
holding my hearts together
my golden hands too
only to break again
over and over
memories
loving wonderful memories
sad painful memories
black awful memories
golden rainbow memories
look at your picture at your shrine
six hundred days
hellfires of grief
dark nights of my soul
continue
six hundred days
you   other goddesses and I
share a sip of cognac
black water too

discovered black water
after you disembodied
know you would
enjoy black water
if still embodied
black water
seems right some how
synchronicity
year of black water dragon
year of black water serpent
six hundred days of black water
seems like my tears should be black
feel black even if
do not look black
six hundred black water days
six hundred days of
black tears

June 25, 2013

# Indispensible

old saying
no one is indispensible
may be true in general
totally false
referring to my intimate other
my soulmate
she is indispensible to me
in whatever form
my small self prefers
my soulmate embodied
even my embodied soul agrees
my higher self has compassion
for my small self
knows old saying
irrelevant in spirit realm
only applies in physical realm
then only in general
to each person
their loved ones are indispensible
once disembodied
painfully true

people may adjust to their loss
but are never the same
no one is indispensible
another old saying
just not true
another lesson in disconnecting
head from heart and soul
lessons in being inauthentic
do not believe old saying

that no one is indispensible
of course
your loved one is indispensible
to you
do not believe old sayings
without wondering about their purpose
do they support living from the head
or living from the heart
a soulful authentic life

sometimes seems acculturation
consists in learning to live
from neck up
educate mind
perhaps exercise body
ignore heart and soul

my beloved is indispensible to me
in whatever form
always forever and beyond

June 30, 2013

# Tip of Iceberg

lot left out of Hellfires I
shared tip of iceberg
not bottom part
most find sanitized version
intense enough
too intense perhaps
grieving mostly a private experience
dark nights of the soul experience
in public people wear their masks
put on their public faces
"just fake it"
epidemic of faking
perhaps sharing tip of
my grief experience
will help others realize
they have company
even if grieving is
a mostly private experience
difficult to share lower part
difficult to reduce experience
into words
lot left out of Hellfires I
lot to be left out of Hellfires II
sharing tip of the iceberg
is enough

July 1, 2013

# Well Meaning Advice

"get on with your life"
well meaning advice
what if the disembodied person is your life
what do you get on with then
grieving
accessing spirit realm

most people are well intended
most are faking it
they knowingly or unknowingly
encourage you to fake it too
put on your mask
your public face
perhaps they are uncomfortable for you
perhaps they are uncomfortable
reminds them they are wearing a mask
faking it
so they offer advice
seem like trite platitudes to me
trite platitudes are
"a dime a dozen"
so put on your mask
your public face
"don't make waves"
"don't rock the boat"
"get on with your life"

July 1, 2013

# Kitten's Nine Lives

thought you had more of
your nine lives left as
my precious embodied kitten
you used up more
than I was aware
taking care of family
work
disembodiments of loved ones
my fumbling around
health issues
still thought you had more
of your nine lives left
you used up your nine lives
much faster than I imagined
awful cancer used
your last embodied life
always thought as one of
Mother's favorite daughters
perhaps you got extra lives
18 or 27 even more
you likely did get extra
used them all
while I was busy pretending
you had more
that Mother would give you more

do not know how many I have used up
wish I had been able to give you
some of mine    perhaps I did
I would have given you my last one
if I knew how

yes I remember you did not
want to be the last one remaining
now I know why
really KNOW why
hellfires of grief
dark nights of the soul
two summary phrases
since words are unable to convey
tears of my heart of hearts
tears of my embodied soul

thought you had more
kitten lives left
I was wrong

wish I knew how to give you
a few of mine
all but the last one
because you did not want
to be the one left behind
when you told me that
I thought I understood
I was wrong
now I know

while it is too late
still wish I could give you
a few of mine
all but the last one
because I remember
now I know why

July 4, 2013

# Two Realms

people lose loved ones all the time
offers no comfort
no comfort in others losses
compassion empathy no comfort
no comfort that loss is inevitable
universality of death of the body
offers no comfort
why would anyone expect it to
pain is universal
suffering is universal
loss is universal
does not lessen
pain suffering loss
feeble attempts
to rationalize
pain suffering loss
grief
away
hyperlogic
head offers no comfort
no compassion no empathy
no healing
purview of the heart embodied soul

Carol Susan's visits with me
in dream time
astral travel when I sleep
provides comfort beyond words
sharing dreams with my soulmate
spiritmate
travels to spirit realm

sometimes my higher spirit self
Carlos Eldon
appears in dreams
most often Carol Susan
Carol Susan being there alone is enough
enough many times over

treasure CS's spirit presence beyond words
miss CS's physical presence beyond words
two realms
two realities
while I much prefer spirit realm
I have unfinished business in physical realm
lessons to learn
messages to deliver
things to do

blessed to share golden dreams
with my beloved
visits to spirit realm
with Carol Susan
provides comfort
beyond
words

July 5, 2013

# Maya's Guardian

setting in our special wicker chair
we picked out long ago
added black cushions
remembering early days
crying feeling sad
lonely without physical presence
of my sweetheart my soulmate
tears falling slowly down my face
heard Maya's little voice
she came laid down
in front of our chair
picked her up
rubbed on her
she started to purr
told her she might not understand
why tears were falling
down my face
Maya's guardian understands
wise old fairy woman
she understands all too well
she has experienced much loss
being guardian of kittens
since cats do not live very long lives
so Maya's guardian understands
has compassion
Maya lays on my lap purring
while I rub her soft fur
feel her tiny fairy kitten body
listening to her purring
tears falling from my eyes
remembering

missing physical person of
my kitten Carol Susan
my soulmate
my companion
Maya jumps on the bed
curls up on her special blanket
takes a nap
her wise old fairy woman guardian
watches over both of us
along with other guardians
tears still falling from my eyes
remembering

thankful I have guardians
thankful for little Maya
laying on my lap purring
thankful for remembering
tears still falling from my eyes
remembering

July 7, 2013

# Crispbread Crackers

when we first came together
I would fix lunch
platter of fruit raw vegetables
cheese and crispbread crackers
we set on our porch
platter between us
sharing food
watching the ocean
sharing the enchantment
the magic of
finding our soulmates

brought crispbread crackers
a year and a half ago
two moves ago
ate one or two
so many memories
wonderful loving memories
stored crispbread crackers
in sealed container
unpacked them after the move
remembered our lunches
on our porch
watching the ocean
sharing the enchantment
the magic
of finding our soulmates

nothing wrong with the crispbread crackers
crispbread crackers are only
crispbread crackers now

like puppy food and spices
they lost their enchantment
their magic
with your disembodiment
no blame
so many memories
wonderful loving memories

I have always known
our love
is
the enchantment
the magic

our love continues
always
forever
and
beyond

July 7, 2013

# Boars Hair Brush

our daughter got the kittens
two baby brushes
boars hair brushes
smaller versions of your brush
you gave to me in 1977
I was combing my hair
complaining it would not lay down
you said "here try my brush"
worked wonderfully
you gave your brush to me
been using it since 1977
thirty six years

unpacking kitten's things
after the move
came upon two baby brushes
smaller versions of your brush
you gave to me in 1977
I held the two little brushes
and cried
remembering when you gave your
boars hair brush to me in 1977
thirty six years ago
so many memories
like when you
gave me your boars hair brush
in 1977
use it almost every day since then
thirty six years
remember each time I use
your brush

your wonderful loving act
may seem like a small thing
giving me your brush
example of your loving acts
symbol of your many loving acts
your many loving ways
so many memories of
other wonderful loving acts

I think about your loving ways
every time I use your brush
thirty six years of memories
of your loving acts
blessed to have so many
wonderful memories
blessed we are making more
golden dreams
old memories and new memories
sustain me since your disembodiment
your boars hair brush
is only one

blessed to experience
your love
sending all my love to you
always
forever
and
beyond

July 8, 2013

# Grandmother Spider's Compassion

after I became aware of
Grandmother Spider as my guardian
started to speculate
where Grandmother Spider
fits in pantheon of goddesses
Grandmother Spider amused
said a human trait
anthropomorphize everything
been wondering if
Grandmother Spider
before or after Kali
hearing Grandmother Spider chuckle
more frightening than Kali's laughter
Grandmother Spider's metamorphosis
into Kali   other goddesses
attempts to humanize Her energy
put a human face on Her
even if the face is a terrible one
still human appearing goddess
Grandmother's face is immense
Her mouth large enough to swallow
whole universes She gave birth to
while giving birth to others
no wonder She chuckled
when I wondered about Her
relationship to Kali
Kali gives birth to Her children
with one hand
eats them with another

frightening goddess
Mother-Crone gone cannibal
frighten enough image
nothing like the
complex compassion of
Grandmother Spider
Her children include universes
birthing and destroying universes
no wonder Her compassion
so complex
no wonder She was amused
by my speculation
Her amusement of short duration
Grandmother wants me to understand
embrace my spider nature
spiders are spirit warriors
spiders do not whine
even very young ones
not sure I make a very good
spider spirit warrior
Grandmother Spider chuckles
agrees says I whine more
than a new born spider
one of Her children
never the less
Grandmother Spider's Compassion

July 17, 2013

# Most Beautiful Flowers

visiting our cottage spring cleaning
looking at things putting things away
organizing old cedar chest
under blankets other things
found a plastic bag
inside folded green florist paper
most beautiful flowers inside
your wedding flowers
pressed preserved
July 30, 1978
one white orchid
you wore for the trip
two red roses one white rose
you carried
perhaps others would not think
they are the most beautiful flowers
almost thirty-five years old
I held your flowers
looked at them with eyes of love
most beautiful flowers
I have ever seen
could feel the love
feel the golden energy
your wedding flowers
stood holding them
crying remembering
feeling our love
almost thirty-fifth wedding anniversary
you have been disembodied 632 days
almost 91 weeks
almost 21 months

our thirty-fifth wedding anniversary in between
glad I found your wedding flowers
most beautiful flowers
I have ever seen
I know you think so too

July 26, 2013

# Days of Observance

each monday I set aside an hour
observance of your disembodiment
usually five pm
set aside last day of each month
observance of monthly anniversary
of your disembodiment
setting here today week ninety-one
thought one day I will convert
hour of observance from
your disembodiment
to your birthday
our wedding anniversary
honor your life
honor our life together
rather than your disembodiment
not ready yet
a lovely inspiration
lovely image
now observe your disembodiment
weekly monthly yearly
your birthday once a year
our wedding anniversary once a year
not balanced
reflects my reality
your birthday our wedding our life together
more worthy of observing
even celebrating
than your disembodiment
not ready yet
concept just occurred to me
reflects my struggle to regain my balance

reconcile myself to my black reality

ironic only celebrated your birthday
our wedding anniversary
once a year
yet observe your disembodiment
weekly monthly yearly
we could have celebrated
your birthday each month
our wedding anniversary each month
I am sorry we did not celebrate
more often
sorry taken me ninety-one weeks
to be inspired with the concept
so I send you all my love
my regrets
because
ninety-one weeks too late

know you like the concept
reveals my fledging attempt at balance

July 29, 2013

25th Wedding Anniversary

# 35th Wedding Anniversary

second anniversary since you left
your physical body
returned to our spirit realm home
embodied we shared many years
many happy days
our wedding thirty-five years ago
one of the very best
many many more
rediscovering our soulmates
deciding to share our lives
side by side
together
courage of spirit warriors
jump into our alchemical crucible
sharing of our souls
reexperiencing our golden cocoon
golden experiences
golden memories

35th wedding anniversary
much like 34th
another year in hellfires of grief
missing physical person of my soulmate
interrupted by golden dreams
still together making new memories
golden dreams
golden experiences
golden memories
wedding of soulmates spiritmates
always forever and beyond

July 30, 2013

Note: 34th Wedding Anniversary, *Hellfires I*, page 116

# Celestial Dream Catcher

made you a golden dream catcher
your 35<sup>th</sup> wedding anniversary present
double soul celestial dream catcher
made of gold ribbons gold thread
Grandmother Spider is black
one of the mysteries
shrouded in darkness
feel with metasenses


making golden dream catcher
realized my present to you
wish hope plea for
more golden dreams
would say I am sorry for being
greedy
would be untrue
I am greedy for more golden dreams
I am not sorry
golden dreams shared with you
most wonderful experiences of my life
since you disembodied
no reason to be sorry
one of few things I celebrate
golden dreams bring golden healing energy
experience of golden joy
portal to sacred spirit realm
and my beloved

I hope you like your present
made with all my love
hopes dreams pleas
greed
Grandmother Spider informs me
wanting to embrace
sacred spirit realm
natural impulse of spirit warrior
not greed
you and old alchemist agree
Grandmother Spider pleased
Her little spider showing promise
you and old alchemist agree


blessed with golden dreams
portal to sacred spirit realm
and my beloved

                                                               July 31, 2013

# Dream Catcher Revelation

making golden double soul dream catcher
two realms overlap in the middle
Grandmother Spider in middle realm
facilitating passage between
two realms
revelation
weaving the middle
suddenly realized
crack between the worlds
looks amazingly like a vagina
stopped working
looked at dream catcher
with new eyes
golden crack between the worlds
new meaning to piercing the veil
born into the spirit realm
heard you laughing saying
"I told you that all along"
Grandmother Spider chuckling too
Grandmother Spider as Cosmic Midwife
assisting her children visit the spirit realm
Grandmother Spider said I was making
slow progress

golden dual soul dream catcher
still unfinished
only middle section complete
powerful revelation
golden dual soul dream catcher

portal to the spirit realm
looks amazing like a vagina
hear you and Grandmother Spider
still giggling

August 1, 2013

# Grief and Four Elements

"We pass through the dark realms of the five elements of earth, fire, air, and space, each one part of the intensely physical experience of grieving." Joan Halifax

been said that
grief proceeds through four elements
earth fire water air

do not understand much about earth
ashes to ashes
dust to dust
my beloved physical remains
in a black marble urn
too much to know about earth
she is no longer of earth
while I still am
more than enough to know about earth

do not understand much about fire
hellfires of grief
burning and burning
more than enough to know about fire

do not understand much about water
black water
tears of grief
black rivers of grief
black oceans of grief
heart of my heart's tears
embodied soul's tears
more than enough to know about water

do not understand much about air
my embodied breathing

my beloved last breath
I am still breathing
my beloved is not
more than enough to know about air

some add space as fifth element
do not understand much about space
understand two realms coexist
access to spirit realm
difficult for me
except in golden dreams
wish I knew more about space

some add metal as fifth element
do not understand much about metal
brittle metal fractures under stress
flexible metal bends under stress
disembodiment of soulmate
ultimate stress
more than enough to know about metal

do not understand much about
grief and the elements
grief proceeds without understanding
not understanding means I have a ways to go
do not understand ways to go either
grief is an experience
understanding may come later
or as I suspect
may never come at all

Note: Joan Halifax quote from **Being with Dying: Cultivating Compassion and Fearlessness in the Presence of Death.** Boston: Shambhala, 2009, page 193.

August 11, 2013

# I Miss You

I miss you
I
miss
you

everyday
I miss your physical being
your physical person

blessed with golden dreams
visits with my beloved
different form
celestial being
golden rainbow angel
energy being

everyday
I miss your physical being
your physical person
my beloved soulmate
embodied

everyday
I miss you
I
miss
you

August 10, 2013

# Not Real Too Real

often does not seem real
that you are not here
not really real
that you disembodied
left your physical body

other times much too real
painfully real horribly real
your beautiful radiant golden spirit
left your physical body
returned to our spirit realm home

know your disembodiment is real
often much too real
intensely real
missing you too much
wanting you too much
grieving for you too much
so I pretend your disembodiment
not really real
pretending does not work
know you disembodied
painfully real horribly real
every moment every hour
every day every week
every month every year
too real
much too real

August 11, 2013

# Two Realms II

do not feel fully of this world
often focus on otherwhere
most of my heart and soul
spirit realm with my beloved
connected to physical realm
family and friends
compassion for others
empathy for others
sympathy for others
do not feel fully of this world
major focus spirit realm
my beloved


still have work to do
in physical realm
unsure what
work learning doing
consists of
some ideas hints
inspirations
sharing my struggles
in hellfires of grief
sharing my experiences
in spirit realm
golden dreams
healing journey
sending love to my soulmate
spiritmate
supporting our daughter

not worried
do not feel fully of this world
no blame
no reason why I would want
to be fully of this world
seekers not fully of this world
dreambody visits spirit realm
remember some golden dreams
spirit realm visits with my beloved
wish I remembered them all
not fully of physical realm
not fully of spirit realm
sleeping in physical realm
dreambody visiting spirit realm
two places at once
way of seekers
no blame
wise person perseveres
success follows
eventually

August 11, 2013

Note: *Two Realms*, **Hellfires II**, July 5, 2013, page 46

# Double Simian Crease

hand analyst pointed out
my double Simian crease
heart line head line
fused as one
both palms
unusual gift markers
extremism intensity stamina
other gifts
energies of heart mind
feelings thoughts
not separate
combined

experience the dark side
in grief
feel the intensity
the extreme heat
hellfires of grief
know I need to burn and burn
unsure about my stamina
or my other gifts

know golden dreams
shared with my beloved
healing gifts
wonderful gifts of love

August 13, 2013

# My Path and I Ching II

consulted I Ching
question continuing on correct path

hexagram 8 union   holding together
image water on earth
union brings good fortune
inquire of oracle again
see if possess
sublimity consistency perseverance

hexagram 27 nourishment   open mouth
careful to take correct nourishment
physical and spiritual
perseverance brings good fortune

changes to hexagram 2 receptive
earth yin feminine
realm of Mother
quiet perseverance brings good fortune
continue being receptive
brings success

August 13, 2013

Note: *My Path and I Ching*, **Hellfires I**, July 31, 2013, page 322

Reference:
Richard Wilhelm (translation) Cary F. Baynes (English translation). **The I Ching or Book of Changes, Volume I.** London: Routledge and Kegan Paul, Ltd., 1951.

# Withered Up II

image of being withered up
not on the outside
not visible with normal eyes
withered up on the inside
see withering with other eyes
shared three energy centers
disconnected
severed
since your disembodiment
physical aspects of
golden cocoon altered
physical energy connections
severed
life force energies
nurturance physical energies
personal power energies
all diminished since
your disembodiment
lower energy cords once connected
dangling dripping energy
gushing at first
now steady drip
more on special days
image of energy dynamics
helps a little
very little
loss is loss
burning is burning
understanding the monster
does not diminish the monster
very much
grief continues to be a dragon

I ride around inside
conversely dragon rides around
inside me
little progress in dropping lower
into dragon's digestive system
nor is dragon dropping
much lower inside me
my feeble efforts to staunch
wounds of severed
lower three energy centers
largely unsuccessful
feel withered wounded damaged
not physical body
energy bodies
lost three lower energy connections
most of my lower three chakra cords
connected to my beloved
now severed
very subtle union remains
spirit realm union
staunching three lower energy centers
very painful process
not very successful
leaking energy
dripping energy
energy cords still seeking their mates
not easy to retract them
not willing to give up their search
three lower energy centers
shriveling up withering up
like a prune
as you would say
missing their mates
missing our shared
physical energies

perhaps shriveling up
withering up
what retraction looks like
does not feel like healing
shriveling up withering up
feels like loss
feels like hellfires of grief
belly of grief dragon
grief dragon in my belly
wonder if I am to be receptive
to three lower energy centers
withering up shriveling up
not sure have much choice
feel diminished in physical realm
three lower energy centers
paradoxically
feel more engaged in spirit realm
compensates for three lower
energy centers being
withered up shriveled up
being an energy "prune"
need to figure how
to obtain increased
energy nurturance power
from spirit realm
open mouth   nurturance
receptive

August 16, 2013

Note: *Withered Up,* **Hellfires I**, March 3, 2013, page 242

References: Barbara Ann Brennan. **Hands of Light: A Guide to Healing Through the Human Energy Field** (1987) and **Light Emerging: The Journey of Personal Healing** (1993). New York: Bantam Books.

# Luck

three lower energy centers
ran out of luck
extremely lucky for many years
then ran out of luck
not wanting to accept
reality of severing
denial
pretending
not really lost
only absent
semantics
did not really
fool myself

possession in great measure
good fortune
golden opportunities
physical realm
many years
then different
black times
much more than
three lower energy centers
ran out of luck
vessel of good fortune
sprang a leak
then broke in two

ran out of luck in physical realm
possession beyond measure continues
more subtle form

spirit realm union
golden dreams
inspirations
being receptive
assures
superior luck
superior good fortune
possession beyond measure
more subtle form
spirit realm union

three lower energy centers
physical realm
still
out of luck
still floundering about
still seeking their mates
still
out of luck

August 16, 2013

# My Birthday 2013

second birthday without you
here in your physical body
know you are here in your
subtle spirit body
somehow just not
quite the same
you always made each birthday
extra special
celebrations filled with love
golden energy
rainbow energy
always looked forward to
birthdays
last year was different
this year was different too
nothing to do with turning
seventy
everything to do with
you were not here in your
physical body
another worst birthday
just like last year
our daughter made the day
as special as possible
under the circumstances
thoughtful cards
thoughtful gifts
special food
day would have been
perfect
but for one exception

you were not here in your
physical body
late at night I wrote in our journal
burned incense
lit candles
drank black water
shared a sip of cognac with you
other goddesses
feeling sad
sorry for myself
you are not here in your
physical body
to share my birthday
you have always been
best birthday present of all
you still are
while no longer present
in your physical body
your spirit presence
best birthday present of all

August 20, 2013

Note: My Birthday 2012: *Hellfires I*: pages 122-123

# Golden Hands II

your golden hands holding
my broken hearts together
helping me heal
you have always held my hearts
in your golden hands
always forever and beyond

aware that my golden hands
are holding yours
holding my broken hearts together
helping me heal
our ancestors golden hands
holding yours and mine
holding our hearts together
always forever and beyond

at first only aware
of your golden hands
holding my broken hearts together
became aware that my higher self
who I call Carlos Eldon
Carlos Eldon's golden hands
joined with yours
holding my broken hearts together
helping me heal
two pairs of celestial golden hands
working together healing
joined by all our ancestors golden hands
working together healing
always forever and beyond

very thankful for golden hands
blessed with all the golden hands
healers all

I am aware golden hands
spirit realm hands
celestial hands
manifested so I can see
experience them
helping me heal
know connected to
celestial energy beings
beings of love
beings of light
my beloved Carol Susan
old alchemist Carlos Eldon
our ancestors
other helpers healers
powerful helpers
powerful healers
holding my broken hearts together
helping me heal
blessed with powerful helpers
powerful healers

August 23, 2013

Note: *Golden Hands*, **Hellfires II**, June 13, 2013, page 32

# Grow Old With Me II

when we first came together
Carol Susan gave me a heart shaped seed
painted on the seed
"Grow Old Along With Me
The Best Is Yet To Be"
for many years I thought
the grow old with me seed
a heart shaped stone
very light stone
not sure when I realized
grow old with me "stone" a seed
perhaps when I placed the
grow old with me seed
on the shrine
my vision certainly been
changed by then
after my discovery
converted my word
to grow old with me seed
realize message not written on stone
written on a seed
seeds transform
miracle of regeneration
seeds become plants
plants bloom flower
produce more seeds
more plants
Carol Susan's promise
given with the grow old with me seed
still being honored
being fulfilled

very different way
from what I expected
hoped for dreamed about
longed for wished for
taken almost 22 months
for me to better understand
Carol Susan's message her promise
given so very long ago
I am growing old
turned seventy this month
Carol Susan is along with me
the best is yet to be
golden dreams
other experiences confirm
Carol Susan honoring her promise
sacred trust given so very long ago
I am the one who took the message
on the grow old with me "stone" literally
now with different vision
"stone" becomes a seed
seed had already transformed
if you look correctly
transformed into golden rainbow dragon
in subtle spirit realm
paradoxically has been there all along
so the message of the grow old with me seed
the best is yet to be is true
just need different vision to understand
always forever and beyond

August 26, 2013

Note: Grow Old With Me: *Hellfires I,* pages 28-29, Nov 24, 2011

# Twenty Two Months

twenty-two months ago
almost 96 weeks ago
667 days ago
worst day of my life
day your beautiful radiant spirit
departed from your physical body
returned to our spirit realm home
reunited with your higher self
my higher self
all our ancestors
many others

October 31, 2011
worst day of my life
667 days ago
days since then
not much better
only golden dreams
dispel some darkness
visits to spirit realm with you
writing **Golden Dreams** with you
dispels some darkness too
collaborating in writing **Golden Dreams**
together
remembering each golden dream
reliving spirit realm visit
dispels hellfires of grief
for a while
sacred work
souls' work
sharing golden dreams with you

writing **Golden Dreams**
together
we will finish writing
111 dreams
put complete draft on your shrine
before October 31, 2013
today we are writing
golden dream sixty-six
*Grandmother Spider*
work of heart
work of soul
sacred work
work of love
healing work
energy of golden dreams
illuminates grief dragon
slowly converts to
golden rainbow dragon of old
golden dreams illuminate
black fires of grief
golden fringes
around black fires
golden sparks within black fires
twenty two months
of black fires

blessed with golden dreams
visits to spirit realm
my beloved

August 31, 2013

Note: *Grandmother Spider*, **Golden Dreams I**,
April 10, 2013, page 106

# Chakra Cleaning

when I shower I clean my chakras
first I ask my helpers for assistance
clean each chakra in turn
starting with root chakra
three whorls of my right hand
counterclockwise
over the chakra
rinse fingers in water
repeat seven times

then charge my chakras
each one in turn
starting with root chakra
three whorls of my right hand
clockwise
over each chakra
repeat seven times
thank my helpers for their assistance

chakras do not seem much cleaner
no more energy
perhaps I am not doing
chakra cleaning correctly
more likely a lot of
darkness
blackness
to clean
not been cleaning my chakras
nearly long enough
expect there is a long way to go
good I have cultivated

perseverance
patience
compassion
know there is
long way to go

August 31, 2013

Note: My thanks to Alberto Villoldo for his description of chakra cleaning. Alberto Villoldo. ***Shaman, Healer, Sage***: **How To Heal Yourself and Others with the Energy Medicine of the Americas.** New York: Harmony Books, 2000, pages 54-55

# Question Why

I often wonder why
why things happen
bad things mostly
answers all unacceptable
one of the mysteries
one of the ten thousand things
fated
destined
accept your fate destiny
not answers
platitudes
nothing more
unacceptable
perhaps I am not asking
right question
perhaps I do not
understand the answers
beyond mortal
human comprehension
unacceptable answer
some god's goddess's will
not an answer
so I keep wondering
seeking
looking behind curtains
beyond the veil
into the mysteries
will I recognize answer
when I find it
hell if I know
will not stop me

from seeking

reminds me of when
I was young boy
liked to take things apart
see how they worked
of course what was given me
no longer worked
certainly no longer worked
after my disassembly
looking back I think
I was wondering
why thing worked
back then too
not how
why things worked
under question how
question why
why do bad things happen
why do things no longer work
I have no better answers now
than I did 60+ years ago
why do things no longer work
because just because
because they are broken
because they stopped working
not answers
then or now
unacceptable

image of little boy
tools in hand
clock parts strewn about
clock no longer working

why
because
broken
not acceptable answer
when I was six years old
reducing clock to pieces
did not work back then
does not work now either
perhaps I am still asking
wrong question
perhaps I do not
comprehend answers
since I refuse to accept
platitudes
perhaps one of platitudes
is the answer
would be ironic
one of platitudes
being the answer
do not think so
answers hidden in mysteries
so I keep seeking
why do bad things happen
why do things stop working
why do people die
why did my beloved
have to die
only fifty seven
fifty seven
why
do not know why
want to know why
need to know why
one of the mysteries

why are there mysteries
if not to explore
seek
enter the mysteries
perhaps by the time
I understand why
I will no longer need
to know why
nowhere near there yet
one of these days
I will know
why
by then I may be
one of the mysteries
too

September 6, 2013

# Hurricane Winds

you gave me sticky note once
about not being able to control the wind
being able to adjust sails
think about that image
as I look at our pictures
they always make me cry
miss you so very very much
your physical person
all my grief work does not change
reality of your disembodiment
wind blows black
hard black winds
hurricane force
driving black rain
take down sails
batten down hatches
strap myself down
ride out storm
as best I can
take on water
tossed about hurricane force winds
ride out storm
as best I can
only adjustment for hurricane
take down sails
ride out storm
as best I can

September 8, 2013

# Loving Acts of Kindness

when embodied
you were a master of loving acts of kindness
encouraged everyone to do
one act of kindness every day
never kept count of all your
loving acts of kindness
far too many
not interested in keeping score
often think about your
loving acts of kindness
try to follow your example
your teaching
experienced your
loving acts of kindness
got a lion's share
many years
not enough years

working on **Golden Dreams**
most healing gifts I have received
sharing gifts of healing
sharing **Golden Dreams**
loving act of kindness
compassion in action
performing loving acts of kindness
following your example
compassion in action
blessed with golden dreams

September 9, 2013

# Self Indulgent

one author says
excessive grief self indulgent

he does not define excessive

implies self indulgence a sin

head defines excessive one way
heart embodied soul another

head believes self indulgence sin
heart embodied soul understand
self indulgence necessary for healing

unfortunately head often rules
buttons down grieving
calls it excessive
grief makes people uncomfortable
so any display excessive
head shames into
swallowing tears
choking back grief
attenuating grief
short circuiting
repressing
throttling back
holding grief tight inside
burying grief in
organs muscles of physical body
creates darkness blocks in
subtle bodies

yes grieving self indulgent
self indulgence necessary
for healing
needs of heart embodied soul
only excessive if you
listen believe your head
rather than your
heart embodied soul

one author says
excessive grief self indulgent
sad victim repressive culture
turned messenger
perpetuation of dis ease
myth that rational thinking
all need to cope heal
not the excessive
self indulgence of grieving

heart embodied soul
know self indulgence
necessary for healing
another word for
compassion

September 12, 2013

# Blessed With Golden Dreams

after your disembodiment
hanging on by a thread
then golden dreams
golden dreams lifeline to spirit realm
golden thread
follow golden thread in dreams
to spirit realm
my beloved
golden dreams
connection between mortal realm
realm of spirits
connection between embodied souls
spirits of spirit realm
connection of soulmatespiritmates
experience merging of
two golden rainbow dragons
in golden dreams
blessed with golden dreams
blessed to remember golden dreams
visits to spirit realm
my beloved
grateful for golden experiences
golden memories
shared with my beloved
blessed with golden dreams

September 14, 2013

# Found Again

we found each other again
remembered our golden cocoon
remembered our golden crucible
remembered our celestial selves
soulmatespiritmates
wonderful physical realm experience
not totally of physical realm
celestial remembering too
made us shine with golden aura
we found each other again
most wonderful discovery
soulmatespiritmates
then you disembodied
felt like I lost you again
part of me knew better
too heartbroken to listen
to whispering of my soul
to whispering of your spirit
too heartbroken to hear
part of me knew
you had changed forms
no longer physical form
spirit form celestial form
angel goddess
golden rainbow dragon
we found each other again
in golden dreams
soulmatespiritmates
always forever and beyond

September 15, 2013

# Wedding Rings

sitting looking at my wedding ring
half rose gold half yellow gold
serpent uroborus
symbol of unity
yin yang together
tai chi
you had it custom made
makes me cry remembering

uroborus eyes worn now
uses other vision
different eyes to see
just as I do

never take off my wedding ring
do not intend to
perhaps seems strange to some
marriage of soulmatespiritmates
made in heaven
spirit realm
celestial realm
transcends mortal physical realm
still some times in my physical body
looking at my wedding ring
makes me cry remembering

your rings in your black marble urn
with your ashes
your physical realm remains
look at them sometimes
your rings

your ashes
makes me cry remembering

I treasure the memories of our
physical realm marriage
time we were embodied
together
far too short
makes me cry remembering

now my experience
golden dreams
your golden spirit presence
whispering when I listen
golden dreams create
new experiences
new memories
blessed with golden dreams
portal to spirit realm
my beloved

still setting looking at my wedding ring
makes me cry remembering

September 15, 2013

# Quest Painting

last year on October 30$^{th}$
finished large painting
loosely modeled after
14$^{th}$ century wood carving
young man in long robe
looks like alchemist
on side of hill
head beyond heavens
into alternative reality
spirit realm
three rainbow bodies
Carol Susan's celestial form
Carlos Eldon's celestial form
Carlos Eldon's astral form
reproduction of wood carving
always appealed to me
represents my quest
reality of my dreams
rather primitive painting
captures my quest
well enough
know I will be successful one day
do not want to wait
know cannot rush
matters of the heart of my heart
my embodied soul
have perseverance compassion
cultivating patience
know I will be successful one day

September 15, 2013

# Amplification

trimming my beard
remembered you telling me
made me look younger
or perhaps I heard you
whispering after all
my physical realm hearing impaired
recommended amplification
perhaps my third ear impaired too
used to say you mumbled
funny first few times not after that
sorry I did not get amplification
when it mattered
would have heard you better
not asked you to repeat yourself
amplification does not matter now
do not sell amplification for third ear
would have bought that long ago
tears open third ear
loss provides amplification
hear you whispering after all

September 15, 2013

# Halloween

Halloween displays everywhere
starts early September   earlier
used to like Halloween
put out bowel of
sour gummy worms
at work
starting October 1$^{st}$
start of Halloween season
decorated little each day
do not like Halloween any more
non holiday for me
no Halloween season any more
no longer holiday for me
October 31$^{st}$ disembodiment day
day of morning
day of grieving

have boxes and boxes
Halloween decorations
large inflatables you gave me
Jack and Sally
Nightmare Before Christmas
October 31, 2010 last Halloween
we celebrated embodied together
Sally would not stay up
kept falling over
rested her in a chair
she was tired
you were too
next Halloween
October 31, 2011

you took your last breath
your beautiful radiant spirit
returned to our spirit realm home
now October 31$^{st}$
not Halloween for me
day of your disembodiment
day of morning
day of grieving
worst day of my life
do not like Halloween
do not like October 31$^{st}$

walking past Halloween displays
remember
Halloween does not exist
for me any more
now disembodiment day
do not need Halloween
my memory frightening enough
do not like
Nightmare Before Christmas
any more either
remember
my own nightmare
call it Disembodiment Day


September 17, 2013

Note: *Day of Disembodiment*, **Hellfires I**, October 31, 2012, page 232
*Disembodiment Day: Year Two*, **Hellfires II**, October 31, 2013, page 132
*Disembodiment Day:: Year Three*, **Hellfires II**, October 31, 2014, page 352

# Dance Floor of Time

when we first met
we did not dance across floor of time
avoiding obstacles in our way
we entered our golden cocoon
floated above floor of time
above obstacles of life
danced in our golden cocoon
our dance of life
above floor of time
beyond time

physical realm changed
seventy year old wounded being
do not dance on floor of time
limp along doing best I can
since your disembodiment

we still float above obstacles of life
dance above floor of time
golden dreams
golden cocoon
dance of life
above floor of time
our spirit realm home
beyond time
soulmatespiritmates
always forever and beyond

September 22, 2013

Note: written after Golden Dream One hundred six
*Fifteen Year Olds*, **Golden Dreams I,**
September 21, 2013, page 169

# Miss You Today

have not written I miss you today
said it to myself often
thought it more often
felt it every moment
of every day
you know since
you live in my heart of hearts
other places
you know without my telling you
tell you anyway
makes me feel a little better
not very much better
little bit better
miss you today
miss you everyday

September 26, 2013

# New Hero Myth

old hero myth medieval
lost power energy radiance
hero slays dragon
rescues damsel in distress
story ends abruptly
killing dragon
wounds hero
often beyond repair
traumatizes maiden
wounding her as well
often beyond repair
development frozen
needed dragon's energy
knowledge wisdom
of the mysteries
dragon knows way
to celestial realm
killing dragon
counterproductive quest
out dated myth
still active

old hero myth
yang way
way of warrior
way of sword
damsel prize
for slaying dragon
both wounded
male female
diminished hollow
I thought it best
if dragon ate hero

not dragon's way
I know
new hero myth
hero befriends
dragon and woman
woman was not in distress
dragon was not hungry
dragons have gotten negative PR
woman seeking companionship
dragon celestial creature
infinite wisdom
willing to share if approached with
respect reverence
male and female
embrace dragon
who shows way to
celestial spirit realm

new hero myth
yin way
male female embrace each other
embrace dragon
dragon shows them the mysteries
new hero myth
shines with luminance
balance
wisdom
delights soul and spirit
way to
celestial spirit realm

March 17, 2013

Note: My thanks to Joseph Campbell, Carl Jung, Marie-Louise von Franz, and others for the images and inspirations.

Note: September 23, 2013: Omitted from **Hellfires I**. Grandmother Dragon my inspiration to add to **Hellfires II** after Golden Dream One hundred eight. *Ancient Teachers*, **Golden Dreams I**, September 23, 2013, page 175

# Seven Hundred Days

seven hundred days
one hundred weeks
twenty three months
since your beautiful radiant spirit
disembodied
returned to spirit realm
seven hundred days
hellfires of grief
dark nights of the soul
journals
poems
black tears
despair
seven hundred days
tonight
burn special incense
new candles
share black water
cognac
with you   other goddesses
seven hundred days
seven hundred nights
missing your embodied
physical being
my physical companion
all my words inadequate
to describe my experience
missing my physical companion
blessed with golden dreams
spirit realm visits with
my beloved

healing golden dreams

new development since
six hundred days
started transforming golden dreams
writing dream poems
**Golden Dreams**
working together
writing
**Golden Dreams**
creates healing energy
golden energy
golden healing
blessed with golden dreams
blessed to be working together
writing
**Golden Dreams**
with my beloved

September 30, 2013

Note: *Six Hundred Days*, **Hellfires II**, June 25, 2013, page 38

Carol Susan with baby lion

# Watching

sitting at a window
watching the world go by
wondering how many others
doing the same
how many wandering around outside
doing the same
wishing they were at home
sitting at a window
watching the world go by

actually
not watching world go by
watching wind
even though
cannot see wind
know wind is present
blowing leaves on trees
trees dancing with wind
watching wind
even though
wind is invisible
watching trees dancing
know wind

go outside
experience wind
beyond my eyes
wind invisible
call the experience
wind

October 1, 2013

# Angels of Mercy

when you became ill
my world got very dark
pretended not to see
figure of death approaching
pretended you would recover
angels of death
angels of mercy
showed up instead to
escort your beautiful radiant spirit
to our spirit realm home
loving Mother welcoming you back
Her Womb portal to spirit realm
when you departed with angels of mercy
part of my embodied soul came along
you and other angels welcomed me
understood I needed to follow
experience your crossing to spirit realm
our higher selves already there to
welcome you home

at first could only see
Kali as dark blue-black death
blood thirsty old hag
taken almost two years
to recognize Kali as
angel of mercy with
fierce warrior's loving compassion
aspect of Kuan Yin

still wonder why angels
not healing angels

instead of angels of death
angels of mercy
struggle to understand
why
no answer adequate
mystery to me

you did not need
angels of mercy
to find your way home
always knew the way
to your higher self
they came along
be with their sister
when you went home
angels of mercy
angels of compassion
angels of love
came to escort their sister home

still struggle with the mystery
why you had to disembody so soon
no answer adequate
mystery to me

blessed to visit with my beloved
angel of mercy
angel of compassion
angel of love
in golden dreams

October 1, 2013

# Making Patacones

when we joined together
you taught me how to
make patacones
Panamian style
we had no tools
used a paper bag
to press plantains
into patacones
you taught me how to
make other Panamian food
enjoyed when I made
Panamian food for you
comfort food from childhood
I loved to make
Panamian food for you
always made you happy

making patacones today
remembering
making patacones for you
I loved making
patacones for you
other Panamian food
always made you happy
made me happy too
miss making Panamian food
for you
wonderful memories
making patacones for you
other Panamian food
always made you happy
made me happy too

October 6, 2013

# Despair

friend told me **Hellfires I**
full of despair
difficult to read
experience of intense despair
I of course agreed
describes my experience
since my soulmate
became sick disembodied
hellfires of grief
dark nights of the soul
despair and anguish
beyond anguish and despair
golden energy of love
soulmatespiritmates
always forever and beyond
golden dreams
slowly healing
anguish and despair
slowly
**Hellfires II** will not lack for
anguish and despair
more balanced
golden dreams
visits to spirit realm
with my beloved
blessed with golden dreams

October 6, 2013

# Red Leaf at Your Shrine

put a red leaf at your shrine
the other day
last year golden ginkgo leaves
year before
did not have a shrine
did not need one
you do not need one
I do
provides some comfort
sharing with you

put a red leaf at your shrine
almost two years since
your beautiful radiant spirit
returned to our spirit realm home
fall does not remind me
of the usual anymore
reminds me of
Disembodiment Day
tears fall harder in fall
approaching
Disembodiment Day
trees lose their leaves in fall
come back in spring
my tears do not care
about seasons
except more fall in fall
approaching
Disembodiment Day

put a red leaf at your shrine
would put a lot more
if they were magic
one red leaf
share fall with you
tell you I miss you
tell you I love you
feel a little better
putting a red leaf at your shrine
sharing fall with you
know you like it too

October 6, 2013

# Contamination

memories of our golden love
mixed with grief's blackness
wonder how long
contamination will last
as long as I am embodied
wonderful golden memories
our life together
our golden love
contaminated by the loss
of your embodied being
contaminated by missing
new experiences
new memories
with your physical realm being

golden dreams
not contaminated
new experiences
new memories
golden memories
golden love
spirit realm visits
with my beloved
golden dreams
slowly healing
little less contamination
know how long
contamination will last
until my last breath
when my embodied soul
returns to our spirit realm home

with my beloved
no other way
burning in hellfires of grief
until all impurities gone
impurities
another name for
imperfections
limitations
remorse regrets
contaminating memories
burning until self forgiveness
self compassion enables
acceptance of limitations
Carol Susan said she did
best she could
within her limitations
powerful example
wonderful teacher
remorse regrets fuel
hellfires of grief
contaminating memory
healing
self forgiveness
compassion for my limitations
slowly healing
accepting my limitations
one by one
slowly healing
work in progress

October 6, 2013

# poems & POEMS

I create
healing poems
not POEMS
not POETRY
not ART
healing poems
heart's tears
translated into words
best I can
not a POET
wounded being
licking my woundedness
with words

Note: Readings include:
John Fox. **Poetic Medicine: The Healing Art of Poem-Making**.
New York: Jeremy P. Tarcher, 1997.

Donald Hall. **The Best Day the Worst Day: Life with Jane Kenyon: A Memoir**. Boston: Houghton Mifflin Company, 2005.

Donald Hall. **Without: Poems**. Boston: Houghton Mifflin Company, 1998.

October 9, 2013

# Not Here Today

not here today
not gone tomorrow
here yesterdays past
705 yesterdays past
who's counting
me damn it
still wondering why
too

wondering why
life's so short
here yesterdays past
gone yesterdays past
here for such a brief moment
gone much too soon

here yesterdays past
gone yesterdays past
I do wonder why
I will until I die
unless of course
I figure it out
before then

October 9, 2013

# Thousand Years

if we lived for
a thousand years
some would start
to get it right
become more fully human
after a few hundred years
maybe more

if we lived for
a thousand years
first few hundred
childhood
next few hundred
adolescence
not expect much
only children
adolescents

time to develop
patience
perseverance
compassion
perfect attributes
talents

not be
snatched
up
at
57

if we lived for
a thousand years
I would not want to
without my beloved

need not worry
life expectancy
only small fraction
of thousand years

I do not worry
about living
a thousand years
without my beloved
visit her often
golden dreams

only seems like
a thousand years
between them
sometimes

October 10, 2013

# Dish Drain Board

washing dish drain board today
remembering after you disembodied
asking our daughter
how dish drain board got so dirty
told me
"mom washed it all the time"
later when you were sick
she washed it
I never noticed
dish drain board got dirty
your standard of clean
few notches above mine
dish drain board never got dirty
until after you disembodied
discovered some little things
only after you disembodied
never realized dish drain board
got dirty
it never did
until after you disembodied
now washing dish drain board
remembering
one of the little things
did not discover nor appreciate
until after you disembodied
now washing dish drain board
makes me sad
makes me cry
remembering

October 20, 2013

Note: see "Little Things" *Hellfires I,* page 297

# Small Clothes

returned to our cottage
spring cleaning visit
understood clearly
time to dispose of your small clothes
gathered them in garbage bag
placed in trash
took to curb
would not seem a difficult task
but it was
disposing of your small clothes
hoped not garbage pickup week
but it was
sad chore
the disposing of your small clothes
know other things
need attending
they can wait
small clothes enough for now
more than enough

October 23, 2013

Note: My thanks to Robert Jordan (Wheel of Time) for the euphemism for underwear

Carol Susan wearing her pollera

# Dream Vision

eyes of the dream
dream vision
spirit eyes
spirit vision
eyes of love
mostly asleep when awake
physical realm
eyes of loss
most awake when asleep
dreamtime
spirit realm
seeing with
dream vision
spirit vision
colors vibrant
golden rainbow energies
now and then
see spirit realm
awake
corner of my eye
veil thins
look directly fades
slow progress
slowly waking up
when "awake"
dreaming awake
spirit vision

October 27, 2013

# Black Lightning

when we met
struck by golden lightning
with rainbow fringes
golden lightning
remembering our eternal love
many life times together

when you disembodied
struck by black lightning
created monster hole
center of my world
looked like the void
black hole
fall in might not find a way out
at least not for a very long time
then changed beyond comprehension
beyond recognition
beyond imagination

remembering being struck by
golden lightning
knowing all our lifetimes together
think I could be less impatient
not desperate for more contact
more golden dreams
more waking dreams
but I am impatient
greedy
desperate for more
remember black lightning too
created black hole

center of my world
center of my heart
black lightning
affected my seeing
affected my memory
blackened my world
blackened my vision
even dragons shocked by
black lightning

golden dreams
antidote to effects of
black lightning
slowly healing
from shock
trauma
memory of being struck by
black lightning
no wonder I am
greedy for more
golden dreams

October 28, 2013

# Disembodiment Day: Year Two

two years ago today your beautiful radiant spirit
left your physical body
returned to our spirit realm home
worst day of my life
hellfires of grief
black night of the soul
hard two years
without your loving physical presence
first year black
swallowed by black dragon named grief
paradoxically swallowed black dragon too
existed within black dragon
black dragon existed within
now and then
golden dream
your golden spirit presence
first year mostly black

second year still black
hellfires of grief
burning and burning
golden dreams
your golden spirit presence
easier to perceive
improved spirit vision
golden rainbow dragon vision
black dragon of grief
may not be smaller
golden dreams

your golden spirit presence
may not be larger
neither may be different
both may be different
end of second year
second black anniversary
observance of disembodiment day
hard two years
without your loving physical presence
shared golden dreams
your golden spirit presence
your loving golden energy
surrounds me
comforts me as nothing else can
healing energy of your spirit love
improved spirit vision
black dragon of grief
may not be much smaller
golden rainbow dragon
seems much bigger
likely same size all along
occluded
by black dragon named grief
now side by side
taking turns in my perception
taking turns in my experience
struck first by golden lightning
when we met
different kind of lightning
transformational
struck by black lightning
when you disembodied
different kind of lightning
transformational

golden dreams
your golden spirit presence
golden rainbow energy
golden love
transformational
transcendent
words not adequate to describe
power of golden dreams
power of your golden spirit presence
power of our love
two golden rainbow dragons
always forever and beyond
best I can do for now
know I will keep trying to
capture our experiences
with words
antidote for black dragon named grief
does not make black dragon disappear
black dragon of grief
will be with me always
as long as I am embodied
your golden spirit presence
shared golden dreams
our golden love
will too

hard two years
miss your physical presence
beyond words
know I always will
blessed with golden dreams
visits to sacred spirit realm
with my beloved
blessed with your spirit presence

Carlos Eldon's too
two golden rainbow dragons
surrounding me with love
thank you

Disembodiment Day Year Two
October 31, 2013

# Last Five Years

one year plus of symptoms
awful diagnosis
two years of awful treatments
disembodiment
two years of loss
two years of hellfires of grief
two years of black nights of the soul
two years of golden dreams
two years of your golden spirit presence

one year plus of concern and love
two years of fear and love
two years of grief and love
hard years
loving years
blessed with golden dreams
blessed with your golden spirit presence
blessed with your golden love

October 31, 2013

# Accidentally On Purpose

are accidents
accidentally on purpose
whose purpose what purpose
mystery to me
what about free will
freedom to fall off the path
not follow one's heart
not listen to one's inner voice
soul's urging soul's purpose
abandon path with heart
free will freedom to fuck up
accidentally on purpose

lost in flatland of frisky dirt
mostly asleep when awake
flatland paradise
ignore wisdom of the dream
embrace pseudobliss of inertia
sloth all the rest
accidentally on purpose

round and round
chasing ones tail
until tired or dizzy
stop or fall down
accidentally on purpose

perhaps frisky dirt
stardust
all along
perhaps free will

accident waiting to happen
accidentally on purpose
of course
mystery to me
perhaps mysteries
accidentally on purpose
too

October 31, 2013
Disembodiment Day

Note: My thanks to Ken Wilber and others for the concept of the flatland.
Ken Wilber for the concept of a flatland of frisky dirt.

# Monkfish

whole monkfish splayed out
on ice in the grocery store
recognized the beast
knew we are brothers
or brother and sister
not sure
felt bad for the creature
giving up its life to be
someone's food
just bought monkfish
few days before
pieces of monkfish
did not recognize
we were brothers
or brother and sister
ate the monkfish
tasty
felt sorry for the monkfish
splayed out on ice
in the grocery store
then thought
we are all food
sooner or later
at least physical realm aspects
Mother gives birth
reabsorbs all her children
eventually
embodied soul transcends
returns to sacred spirit realm
perhaps different kind of food
mystery to me

only physical parts
food for Mother Nature
sooner or later

spirit exempt
from reabsorption

felt compassion
empathy
for the monkfish
splayed out on ice
in the grocery store
we are related
after all

gave thanks for the piece of monkfish
I ate the other day
gave thanks to all monkfish
for being food
we are all food
sooner or later

except the part
that goes free

November 1, 2013
All Saints Day
Day of the Dead

# Day and Night

nights often golden
golden dreams
days often black
hellfires of grief
reversed yin and yang
asleep during day time
under a cover of blackness
awake at night
splendor of golden dreams
visits to spirit realm
my beloved
not much of a spirit warrior
discouraged by darkness of day
hellfires of grief
day time experience

nights experience golden dreams
sometimes hellfires of grief
invade the night
black dreams
nightmares
golden dreams spill
into the day bringing
golden healing energy
presence of my beloved

nightmares remind me of
physical realm reality
lest some how I forget
my waking nightmare
unforgettable

sometimes overwhelmed by
golden dreams
presence of my beloved
blessed with golden dreams
presence of my beloved

November 5, 2013

# Second Book

our second book arrived from printer
thinking about our two books
one describes day
black hellfires of grief
other describes night
golden dreams
same time period
describe different realities
golden dreams stream into day
hellfires of day
burn in dream time
nightmares
only a few
living nightmare awake
miss your physical embodied being
blessed with golden dreams
keep me from crisping
in hellfires of grief
golden dreams
keep me from withering
golden rainbow energy
your spirit presence
your golden love
healing golden dreams
possession beyond measure

put our second book
on your shrine
along with first
two books
description of my experience

glimpses of your experience
visits to our spirit realm home
with my beloved
reduced into words
words not adequate
have to be enough
best I can do

our next two books
on your shrine too
Hellfires II
Golden Dreams II
each partially complete
continuations of
Hellfires I
Golden Dreams I

blessed with golden dreams
visits to spirit realm
with my beloved

November 11, 2013

Note: *First Book*, **Hellfires II**, June 4, 2013, page 30

# Healing Poems

healing poems
licking my woundedness
with words
lovely concept
requires endless supply of words
very slow healing
licking my woundedness
with words

golden dreams
golden rainbow dragon
surrounding my woundedness
golden healing energy
words not needed
golden love
golden healing

golden dreams
reduced to words
retain some
golden healing magic

blessed with golden dreams
possession beyond measure
visits to spirit realm
with my beloved

November 13, 2013

# Counting My Blessings

counting my blessings
counting my losses
my greatest blessing
my greatest loss
counting my blessings
over and over
counting my losses
over and over

results of my counting
always the same
my greatest blessing
my greatest loss
when counting
my physical realm
blessings
physical realm
losses

spirit realm
only blessings
no losses
golden dreams
your golden spirit presence
spirit realm
only blessings
no losses
do not remember
every golden dream
some fade upon waking
blessed to remember

golden dreams
blessed to experience
your golden spirit presence
blessed with golden dreams
ones I remember
your spirit presence
never absent
treasure your spirit presence
blessed with
your golden spirit presence
golden dreams
visits to spirit realm
with you
my greatest blessings
always forever and beyond

November 15, 2013

# No Contest

thinking about how you used to tell me
I would never know just how much
you love me
thinking about how much
I love you
know you know just how much
then another thought
we could have a contest
who loves who the most
had to chuckle
thinking such a foolish thought
not a contest
heard you chuckling
about my idea too
my counting weighting measuring
physical realm rational
head affliction
heard you whisper
"we will call it a tie"
you were chuckling too
our energy merges in golden dreams
illuminates my understanding
seeing from your spirit eyes
feeling your golden hands
holding my broken hearts
helping me heal
I have some idea
just how much you love me
no contest
enough
more than enough

beyond enough
a love eternal
always forever and beyond

thank you
for indulging me with my
silly contest idea
"we will call it a tie"
lovely elegant solution
our spirit realm love
beyond my rational counting
weighing measuring ways
two golden rainbow dragons
celestial uroborus
golden rainbow energy
hard to tell where one starts
other leaves off
happened in physical realm too
beyond words
abundance in great measure
beyond measure
no contest

November 16, 2013

# Fireplace in Chester

remembering our fireplace in Chester
we would start a fire
gather blankets
start our own fire
more intense
more memorable

remembering our fireplace in Chester
remembering our fire
we took our fire when we moved
miss our fireplace in Chester a little
miss our fire beyond words
days turn black
nights without golden dreams
black nights too
sun moon stars on strike
our fire is not gone
transformed
our fire went with you
when you moved
spirit realm address
subtle spirit fire
visit in golden dreams

remembering our fire
physical realm fire
inside alchemical crucible
external fire not needed
alchemical fire of our love

remembering our fireplace in Chester
remembering our fire
now alchemical fire of our love
coexisting with
black hellfires of grief
wonderful remembering
our physical realm fire
blessed experiencing our fire
transformed in subtle spirit realm
subtle spirit fire
experienced in golden dreams
visits to spirit realm
with you
blessed with golden dreams
spirit realm fire
shared with you

November 21, 2013

# Cats Playing

watching Maya and Merlin
playing with the box
brown packing paper
after I removed copies of
**Golden Dreams**
enjoyed watching them play
cats live in the moment
wondered if they knew
significance of box
brown packing paper
had held copies of
**Golden Dreams**
sad kittens did not meet
your embodied being
wondered if cats grieve
remember they visit your shrine
from time to time
put their paws on your picture
the large one on the wall
smell the purple orchid
other things
never play with objects
on the shrine
like they do other places
including the bookshelf
only a few feet away
seems they understand
significance of the shrine
likely see your presence
better than me
sometimes they look around

as if seeing into otherwhere
I suspect they can
better than me
I enjoy watching them play
with the box
brown packing paper
held copies of
**Golden Dreams**
left the box
packing paper
on the floor

I know cats dream from
watching Maya and Merlin
sleeping
chasing dream world food or
perhaps running for fun
running in their dreams
little legs working
sometimes with
claws extended
tails puffed up
think they have nightmares
just like me
hope they are blessed with
golden dreams too

November 22, 2013

Hollywood Beach, Florida
2010

# Thanksgiving Three

Thanksgiving 2011
worst Thanksgiving of my life
too raw to be thankful for much
remember other Thanksgivings
thankful shared them with you

Thanksgiving 2012
second worst Thanksgiving of my life
remember other Thanksgivings
thankful shared them with you
thankful for golden dreams
visits to spirit realm shared with you

Thanksgiving 2013
third worst Thanksgiving of my life
remember other Thanksgivings
thankful shared them with you
thankful for golden dreams
thankful for your golden spirit presence

blessed with golden dreams
your golden spirit presence
embodied and spirit
helpers healers

November 24, 2013

"Thanksgiving 2011": ***Hellfires I,*** page 30
Thanksgiving 2012: "Holidays are Hell": ***Hellfires I***, page 145

# Black Thanksgivings

Thanksgiving 2009
we shared in your hospital room
trying to make the best of it
you too sick to eat much
I too sick at heart to eat much
Taryne Jade on her way home

Thanksgiving 2010
we shared at our cottage
by then you knew
horrible cancer reoccurred
confirmed in December before
your last embodied Christmas

Thanksgiving 2011
your physical being gone
you disembodied last day of October
your beautiful radiant spirit
returned to our spirit realm home
worst Thanksgiving of my life

we shared many wonderful Thanksgivings
starting in 1977
blessed with abundance in great measure
thankful grateful beyond words
so many wonderful Thanksgivings
so many reasons to be thankful

starting 2009 Thanksgivings
darker and darker
then turned black

blackness often obscures
wonderful Thanksgivings of old
Black Thanksgivings prevail
coat my memories with blackness
do not know how it
could be any other way
not totally successful distorting
our Thanksgivings of old
remember our many blessings
thankful every day
remember last five Thanksgivings
very different memories
two dark Thanksgivings
three black Thanksgivings
do not know how it
could be any other way
Black Thanksgivings
missing your embodied being
missing you
thankful for golden dreams
your golden spirit presence
blessed beyond measure
grateful beyond measure
do not know how it
could be any other way

November 25, 2013

# Spoiled Rotten

indulged
well loved
intensely loved
fiercely loved
some might even say
spoiled rotten
I agree
wonderful experiences
wonderful memories
being spoiled rotten
by my beloved

I miss your physical being
spoiling me rotten with love
still being spoiled
continues beyond
your disembodiment
changed forms
harder to see
harder to feel
more subtle
feel your presence
golden rainbow spirit energy
surrounding me
your golden love
spirit embrace
spoiled by an angel
goddess
golden energy being
golden dreams
golden love spoiling me

always forever and beyond
blessed to be spoiled rotten
indulged
well loved
intensely loved
fiercely loved
spoiled rotten
with your
eternal love

November 26, 2013

Note: See "Grandmother" *Golden Dreams*, page 64

February 2, 2011

# School of Grief

no applications
no entrance exams
only perquisite
disembodiment of a loved one
then enrollment automatic
may pretend school does not exist
enrolled anyway
most painful school
most difficult school
much to learn
many teachers
learn language of tears
language of grief
bereavement loss
hearts broken in two
over and over
language of healing
most difficult language of all
lifelong learning
no graduation
no certificate
no diploma
graduate to spirit realm
celestial school
cannot say much
about celestial school
only had glimpses
do know
enrollment automatic

November 26, 2013

# All Golden Dreams

want all dreams to be golden dreams
visits to spirit realm with my beloved
know being greedy
golden dreams sustain me
not remembering dreams discouraging
not having more golden dreams discouraging
wisdom of the Self prevails
each dream's timing ideal
understand the concept even agree
still want all dreams to be golden dreams
small self not wise
miss my embodied soulmate
only golden dreams provide enough love
since your disembodiment
nightmares
housekeeping dreams
other dreams
remind me still in physical realm
know your spirit presence
surrounds me
when not experiencing golden dreams
feel your golden spirit love
hear your soft whispers
from time to time
know the other dreams
assist keeping me grounded
focused on work left to do
understand all of that
still want every dream to be a
golden dream
all golden dreams

know it will not be so
hold golden dreams in my heart of hearts
other dreams likely reside there as well
perhaps they are golden too
in their own way
seems unlikely
even if true
serve other purposes
wish all dreams were golden dreams
know it will not be so
grateful beyond measure
for the golden dreams
I remember
visits to spirit realm with my beloved
blessed with golden dreams

December 1, 2013

"...every dream that a person remembers is a 'best fit' — *the best possible dream* for that person to have had at that particular moment."

Jeremy Taylor. *The Wisdom of Your Dreams: Using Dreams to Tap Into Your Unconscious and Transform Your Life*. New York: Jeremy P. Tarcher/Penguin, 2009, page 153.

# Sometimes

sometimes
licking my woundedness with words
not enough

sometimes
golden dreams
not enough

sometimes
when nothing else is enough
I lick my woundedness with tears

sometimes
licking my woundedness with tears
not enough
either

perhaps sometimes
comes more often than
sometimes

sometimes
licking my woundedness with hellfires of grief
almost feels like enough
sometimes

December 4, 2013

Note: Written at our cottage day before appointment at
Clerk's Office, Circuit Court, Probate Division

# Few Minutes Into Forever

one minute you were fine
next minute you were sick
next minute you were very sick
next minute you were gone
disembodied
your physical body gone
only a few minutes
few minutes into forever
seems so unreal
your physical being no longer here
seems all too damn real too
paradoxically
all too damn real
me powerless helpless
to change reality
can not have what I want most
miss your physical being intensely
so very lonely without your
physical being
reduced to ashes
comforted by golden dreams
only remember a few
comforted by your spirit presence
very subtle spirit presence
comforted by your whispered messages
very soft whispers
no lack of direct experience grieving
intense experience
few minutes into forever

December 5, 2013

Note: Written at our cottage after filed Carol Susan's will

# Sneaking Up On Paradox

remember then forget
over and over
not constrained by veil
forget my quest not to pierce veil
quest to remember
already travel to and from spirit realm
veil non existent
except keep forgetting
perhaps veil another name
for my forgetting mechanism
spirit realm not behind veil
my memory veiled
active forgetting
powerful forgetting mechanism
forget most of my dreams
forget most of my waking experiences
more asleep than awake
veil metaphorical blinders
remember then forget
over and over
now and then think I have been successful
sneaking beyond paradox
only to forget
always known how
keep forgetting
over and over
perhaps I spend too much time
sneaking up on paradox
attempting to
sneak beyond paradox
playing with words concepts

my forgetting mechanism
seems to enjoy watching me
sneaking up on paradox
only to forget
already beyond paradox
just do not remember
excellent forgetting skills
so sneaking up on paradox
again

December 8, 2013

# Looking At Memories

in our garage looking in boxes
searching for papers
finding memories
sweet and bitter memories
many many memories
sweet memories we made together
bitter as you are no longer embodied
to reminisce with me
open boxes
hold memories in my hands
reminisce with your spirit being
you are very indulgent
watching me looking at memories
reminiscing with you
boxes and boxes of memories
grateful for so many memories
sad your physical being no longer able to reminisce
used to fantasize how we would sit
looking in boxes when we got old
not what I expected
reminiscing with subtle energy being
thankful for your indulgence
looking in boxes
looking at memories
reminiscing with you

December 9, 2013

# Changing Forms

intense impact of your
changing forms
beloved physical being
beloved spirit being
wish to fully celebrate your spirit being
miss your physical being too much
to fully experience your spirit form
without my memory physical senses
reminding me
your physical form missing
know your spirit fills space left empty
by your disembodiment
miss my physical companion too much to
fully appreciate your spirit form
physical being once primary
spirit being now primary
miss your physical form
not fully adjusted to your
changing forms
even though we have
been spiritmates together
always forever and beyond
miss my embodied soulmate
hope to fully celebrate your spirit form
someday

December 12, 2013

# Advisor to Companion

used to talk about death as an advisor
look quickly over my left shoulder
catch glimpse of death
words   intellectual concepts
since your disembodiment
death no longer my advisor
nor intellectual concept
no need to look
over my left shoulder
quickly or otherwise
to catch glimpse of death
since your disembodiment
death moved from now and then
to here and now
constant and always
death lays across my shoulders
an invisible black bone scarf
casting dark black shadows
across my heart
while I struggle to retain balance
equilibrium
struggle to better perceive
your subtle spirit presence
remains unchanged
except
no longer confined
contained by your physical body
while death drapes across my shoulders
a dark companion casting shadows
your golden rainbow presence
fills my heart of hearts

two companions coexisting
of the two you are so much stronger
death restricted to physical realm
physical realm companion
you and I are companions
soulmatespiritmates
always forever and beyond

December 19, 2013

Note: My thanks to Carlos Castaneda for the concept
death as an advisor
Carlos Castaneda. *Journey to Ixtlan: The Lessons of Don Juan*,
New York: Simon and Schuster, 1972,
Chapter 4: Death Is An Advisor, pages 46-57

# Dragon Named Grief

image of dragon named grief changing
name changing too
dragon named grief also named
Carlos Eldon
Carlos Eldon the small
one of his names
not his true name
close enough for now
strangely comforting realization
dragon named grief also named
Carlos Eldon
golden heart of hearts
Carlos Eldon the small
also holds small portion of
Carol Susan's golden spirit
in my heart of hearts
which Carol Susan gave me
to keep me company
when I get very sad
forget to look into my heart of hearts
forget all I need to do
open my spirit eyes
use my spirit vision
instead of my physical eyes
instead of my physical vision
intensely miss your physical being
remember your spirit being not lost
remembering sustains me
experiencing your golden spirit
golden rainbow dragon
named Carol Susan

one of your names
not your true name
close enough for now
shrinks dragon named grief
converts to dragon named
Carlos Eldon
as if bite off some darkness
convert to golden love
two golden rainbow dragons
always forever and beyond

December 19, 2013

Note: "A Dragon Named Grief" ***Hellfires of Grief: Love Poems*** ,
October 31, 2012, page 130

# Sharing Winter Solstices

thirty six Winter Solstices shared
first thirty three embodied together
last three shared our new way
mixture of sadness and wonder
spoiled by your embodied sharing
treasure sharing with your spirit
before had both now only one
no small thing sharing with
your spirit
no small thing sharing with
my embodied soulmate
celebrating Winter Solstice 2013
with my celestial spiritmate
morning loss of my soulmate
Winter Solstice 2009
you were very sick
flew from Florida to Johns Hopkins
emergency surgery to prolong your
embodied life
long enough for major surgery
early 2010
Winter Solstice 2010
our cottage in Virginia
heartbroken Winter Solstice
cancer had returned
Winter Solstice 2010
your last embodied
last embodied Christmas
New Years
Lunar New Years

disembodied before
Winter Solstice 2011
worst Winter Solstice of my embodied life
too raw numb shriveled
heartsick soulsick
grief struck
to understand our new way of sharing
only perceive blackness
Black Winter Solstice of 2011
Winter Solstice of 2012
second worst of my embodied life
Winter Solstice 2013
third worst
now look backwards
Winter Solstices of old
other holidays as well
holidays of old spent
mix of looking
backwards
forward
celebrating
together
we shared reminisces
future plans dreams
part of celebration
shared together
Winter Solstice good time to
share reminisces
future plans hopes dreams
part of celebration
mostly look backwards now
write in our journal
do not look forward much
do not celebrate holidays

like we shared together when
you were embodied
perhaps could celebrate more
look forward more
if I could better remember
my spirit realm visits
Winter Solstice 2013
remembering holidays gone
Winter Solstices of old
wishing for golden dreams
improved spirit realm memory
realize I am doing best I can
as you say
within my limitations
my limitations seem much larger
than ever before
my resilience sorely challenged
tested found wanting
raw diminished
mostly looking backward
Winter Solstice 2013
remembering Winter Solstices of old
shared with my embodied soulmate
reminiscing more than looking ahead
some dreaming of future holidays
dreaming of my improved
spirit realm senses
improved metasenses
memory for spirit realm visits
so I could better share holidays
our new way of sharing
our third Winter Solstice
shared our new way
doing the best I can

within my limitations
know you and Carlos Eldon agree
Happy Winter Solstice 2013
our new way of sharing
across realms

Winter Solstice 2013
December 21, 2013

# New Way of Sharing

struggling to understand our
new way of sharing
struggling to fully embrace our
new way of sharing
know not really new
spiritmates
always forever and beyond
eternal love
eternal sharing
embodied sharing of soulmates
sharing I miss
spoiled by our embodied sharing
not struggling to understand our
new way of sharing
struggling to adjust to loss of our
embodied way of sharing
experience our new way of sharing
golden dreams
your subtle spirit presence
soft whispers now and then
struggling to fully embrace
new way of sharing
memories of our embodied sharing
comfort me
experiences embodied together
best memories of my life
perhaps new way of sharing
will need to share with
our old way of sharing
at least until I get better at
fully embracing our

new way of sharing
do not know how long
will be required
as long as necessary
as much time as needed
as much time as available
as the I Ching advises
no blame
I will fully embrace
sharing in
new way
old way
together
soulmatespiritmates
always forever and beyond

December 22, 2013

Note: My thanks to Doreen Virtue for her words and works of wisdom.

"Our relationships with our loved ones don't end with their death. The relationship merely changes form. As a psychotherapist and clairvoyant medium, I help my clients maintain healthy relationships with their loved ones on the other side. Healthy post-death relationships are important for the sakes of souls on both sides of the veil of death." page 97

Doreen Virtue. ***Healing with the Angels: How the Angels Can Assist You in Every Area of Your Life.*** Hay House, 1999.

# Christmas 2013

third Christmas
since your beautiful radiant
golden rainbow spirit
returned to the spirit realm

Christmas 2011 at our cottage
black Christmas
first after your disembodiment
worst Christmas of my life

Christmas 2012 at our cottage
Maya and Merlin
four months old
rode from Iowa City to Virginia
spent their first Christmas
at our cottage
fuzzy little healers
second worst Christmas of my life
enjoyed watching kittens
explore our cottage

Christmas 2013 Coralville Iowa
third worst Christmas of my life
kittens got a Christmas tree
call it Winter Solstice tree
no ornaments few lights
kittens enjoy their tree
got a remote control mouse
enjoy wrapping paper
tissue paper even more
laying by the fire most of all

enjoy watching kittens at play
enjoy watching kittens at sleep
carry them around sometimes
hold their furry little bodies
close to my heart
they are much better
living in the moment
than me
I remember other Christmases
wonderful Christmases
shared with my embodied soulmate
last three Christmases painfully different
struggling to share with my spiritmate
learning from kittens
excellent teachers
teach by example
just like you
healers too
I am a difficult student
remembering more than
experiencing the moment
remembering Christmases
gone

remembering my best present
grateful for abundance beyond measure
golden dreams
your golden presence
new way of sharing

physically embodied ones
our daughter her kittens me
made the best of Christmas 2013
your physical presence intensely missed

your spirit presence
golden dreams
our new way of sharing
best presents of all
always forever and beyond

Christmas 2013
December 25, 2013

# Forgotten Golden Dreams

know I have more golden dreams
than I remember
only remember a few
treasures beyond measure
words inadequate
two dimensional descriptions of
golden rainbow spirit realm
suspect sometimes
experience of dreamtime
journeys to spirit realm
only remembered by
my embodied soul
only aspect capable of remembering
all radiant spirit realm experiences
my small self attempts
to capture experiences
using words concepts images
when unsuccessful    forgets
experiences reside in my embodied soul
my heart of hearts
just out of reach of my small self
happens to my waking journeys
to spirit realm too
spirit realm experiences still exist
just beyond recall beyond memory
forgotten not gone
forgotten golden dreams
still healing
just beyond recall beyond memory
still healing

December 26, 2013

Note: My thanks to Jeremy Taylor for his valuable writing on forgetting dreams (***Wisdom of Your Dreams***, 2009, pages 84-88)

# Careful Wishing

in days gone by
I would complain to Carol Susan
about my underdeveloped metasenses
always studying reading seeking
the key a key
something to open the door
Carol Susan would say
"be careful what you wish for"
she already knew
what I did not discover
until many years later
my seeking had been a hobby
past time now and then pursuit
lacking fire lacking passion
poorly focused
more head than heart
after Carol Susan's disembodiment
I realize what she means by
"be careful what you wish for"
I was not careful in my wishing
more than enough fire now
hellfires of grief
invisible black fire
too bright to see
too hot to focus
still seeking
blindly looking
for the key a key
the door a door
no longer a hobby
on longer part time

now sacred quest
quest I mistakenly thought
to pierce the veil
open the door to
sacred spirit realm
heart of my heart's quest
embodied soul's quest
my new life's work
vision cleared enough to discover
veil is my forgetting
door internal
highly skilled at forgetting
remembering mechanism blocked
forgetting mechanism very effective
life time of practice
expert at forgetting
beginner at remembering
no longer my hobby
heart of my heart's desire
sacred quest to remember
nothing wrong with my metasenses
something wrong with my remembering
something wrong with my forgetting
something wrong with my wishing too
not careful what I wished for
as I Ching advises
wise person perseveres
not wise in my wishing
persevere in my quest to remember
nothing wrong with my metasenses
something wrong with my remembering
more than enough fire now

December 31, 2013

# New Years 2014

twenty thirteen
second full calendar year
without your physical being
to share end of one year
beginning of another
792 days
113 weeks
26 months
2 years 2 months
since your beautiful radiant spirit
disembodied
returned to our spirit realm home
holidays all different now
new years no exception
kept few of our traditions
added very different ones
light candles burn incense
share black water cognac
with you and other goddesses
held some money at midnight
tradition I learned from you
put some money on your urn
at your shrine
share our tradition
know you do not need money
know you like our sharing
remembering our traditions
sending you my love
feeling your golden presence
your golden love in return
wrote in our journal after midnight
remembering crying
sharing black water cognac
telling you how much I miss

your embodied physical being
you of course already know
need to tell you anyway
helps a little
listening to "A Love Eternal"
makes me cry
listen to it multiple times
like I always do
listen for your soft whispers
feel your subtle golden presence
sharing New Years 2014
in your new form
792 days
113 weeks
26 months
2 years 2 months
since your beautiful radiant spirit
disembodied
I miss your physical being too much
I know I always will
blessed with abundance beyond measure
golden dreams
your golden rainbow spirit presence
your whispers from time to time
sharing New Years 2014
old traditions new traditions
remembering old experiences
making new memories
sharing New Years 2014
with you

January 1, 2014

Note: *New Years 2012*, **Hellfires I**, page 70
New Year 2013, **Hellfires I**, page 182

Peter Sterling, *A Love Eternal*, **Harp Magic,**
Harp Magic Music, 1993/2004, www.harpmagic.com

# Fortune Cookies

New Years Eve 2014
ate Chinese food
long time shared tradition
fortune cookie fortune
"You will have good luck in your personal affairs."
New Years Day
ate leftover Chinese food
another long time shared tradition
fortune cookie fortune
no physical fortune
invisible fortune
spirit realm fortune
possession beyond measure
wonderful spirit realm fortune
possession beyond measure
golden dreams
your golden spirit presence
perhaps good fortune for 2014
improved memory of
spirit realm visits
shared with you
more golden dreams
more subtle messages
new experiences
new memories
fortuitous spirit realm fortune

January 1, 2014

# Spirit Realm Resident

small embodied self
not spirit realm resident
like my higher Self
small self wants to tag along
visit now and then
perhaps more often
may not be correct attitude
tagging along sounds parasitic
may not be worthy attitude
not a superior attitude
will consult I Ching
ask correct question this time
not am I on right path
could be standing on right path
same place very long time
no movement no progress
correct question proper attitude
to make progress on my quest
regain dragon vision
dragon energy
remember my visits to sacred spirit realm
with my beloved and my higher Self
do not care if parasitic
visits to spirit realm home
know my embodied soul remembers
most likely resides both places at once
always forever and beyond
small dragon cannot remember
only glimpses now and then
not enough
must be something wrong
with my attitude

January 2, 2014

# Superior Attitude & I Ching

what is superior attitude to
approach sacred spirit realm
changing hexagrams
first number eleven   peace
image heaven below earth above
heaven on earth
changing as heaven sinks
into earth
do not resist change
submit to fate
changes to number twenty six
taming power of the great
image heaven below mountain above
heaven within the mountain
hidden treasure
store energy
strengthen character
maintain virtue in words and deeds
as above so below
correspondence in heaven
heaven within
perseverance furthers

January 4, 2014

Note: Superior translates to ideal or attitude most likely to lead to good fortune, most fortuitous attitude, best attitude to adopt for success.

Reference:
Richard Wilhelm (translation) Cary F. Baynes (English translation). **The I Ching or Book of Changes, Volume I.** London: Routledge and Kegan Paul, Ltd., 1951.

# Enduring Relationship

"If you would have your relationship endure,
fix your mind on an end that endures."
Wu Wei

I Ching advised studying
sayings of antiquity
enduring relationship
one I like best
superior advice
establish goal of permanently
maintaining relationship
commitment for relationship to endure
ensures success
unsure referring to
eternal relationship
perhaps
I Ching contains
wisdom of antiquity
conformation from I Ching
sacred spirit realm
other sources
enduring relationship
soulmatespiritmates
always forever and beyond

January 5, 2014

Note: My thanks to Wu Wei. *I Ching Wisdom: Volume One: Guidance from the Book of Changes.* Los Angeles, California: Power Press, 2005, page 99

# Lake of Longing

"When was the last time you cried
lost tears into the lake of longing?
Sipped inspiration from the pool of wonder?
Or rose, victorious, like a phoenix from the ashes?"
Angi Sullins

reading **A Knock at the Door** again
came to the part about
lake of longing
cried again
same answer again
today
every day
799 days
many days before
lake of longing
very large
easily mistaken for ocean
ocean of longing
today
every day
799 days
many days before

inspiration
call them golden dreams
subtle whispers messages
presence of golden rainbow dragon

no sign of phoenix
only ashes
lake of longing

January 8, 2014

Note: Words, pictures, & CD by Angi Sullins & Silas Toball.
*A Knock at the Door*. Portland, Oregon: Amber Lotus Publishing, 2008

# Eight Hundred Days

eight hundred days
since your beautiful radiant spirit
returned to our spirit realm home
eight hundred days
since your disembodiment
eight hundred days
burning and burning
hellfires of grief
eight hundred black days
eight hundred black nights
worst eight hundred days
of my embodied life
except for golden dreams
your golden spirit presence
helping me heal
others also helping
embodied and disembodied
looking back before 800 days
possession in great measure
treasure our experiences memories
shared embodied together
companions soulmates
loving memories comfort me
remember you telling me
my love was enough
when I could not do more
your disembodiment much too soon
our love could not over come
your disembodiment
death to your physical body
looking back over 800 days
golden rainbow cocoon exists
perfect in spirit realm
possession beyond measure

always forever and beyond

at 800 days struggling
to adjust to your transformation
subtle spirit realm form
golden rainbow dragon mother goddess
goddess of compassionate healing
holding my hearts in
your golden rainbow hands
spirit realm holding
spirit realm healing
slowly healing
your old physical realm creature
Carlos Eldon
ancestors
others helping

at 800 days looking back
read **Golden Dreams Hellfires I**
as we work on **Golden Dreams II**
new experiences new memories
golden dreams
wonderful spirit realm visits
translating spirit realm experiences
into words best I can
you Carlos Eldon ancestors
tell me it is good enough

Hellfires II now halfway completed
111 of 222
translating hellfires of grief
translating my slow healing
into words best I can

at 800 days looking backwards
looking forward as well
golden dreams
spirit realm experiences

black hellfires of grief
competing with
golden rainbow heartfire
both fires invisible to usual seeing

no grief without love
no love without grief
possession in great measure
love loss grief

spirit realm
possession beyond measure
golden love
no loss
no grief
compassion for embodied souls
possession beyond measure

at 800 days
experience
loss of possession in great measure
transforming into
possession beyond measure
soulmatespiritmates
always forever and beyond
blessed with
possession beyond measure
eternal love

Eight Hundred Days
January 9, 2014

Note: *Seven Hundred Days.* **Hellfires II,** September 30, 2013, page 110
*Six Hundred Days,* **Hellfires II**, June 25, 2013, page 38
*Five Hundred Days,* **Hellfires I,** March 17, 2013, page 260

# Possession Beyond Measure

I Ching hexagram called
possession in great measure
our first hexagram
when our embodied beings first met
first hexagram
possession in great measure
very fortuitous accurate
wisdom of I Ching
when approached with reverence
I Ching accurate
while you were embodied
with your disembodiment
renamed our first hexagram
possession beyond measure
very fortuitous accurate
wisdom of I Ching
applied to subtle spirit realm
measures apply to physical realm
sacred spirit realm beyond measure
renaming our first hexagram
necessary after your transformation
miss possession in great measure
blessed with possession beyond measure

January 13, 2014

# Struggling

become exhausted with struggling
adjusting to our new relationship
your new form
struggling
miss your old form
your physical being too much
know I always will

struggling between
darkness of physical realm
after your disembodiment
absence of your physical being
hellfires of grief
contrasted to
golden rainbow radiance of spirit realm
your new form
your always forever and beyond form
golden dreams
your spirit presence
two realities coexisting
hellfires of grief mixture
heart fires of love
black fires of loss
do not know what healing feels like
perhaps two realities coexisting
absence of struggling
long way to go

January 13, 2014

# Alchemy of Grief

writing in our journal at 116 weeks
thinking about images
invisible black bone scarf
draped over my shoulders
around my neck
image of death
near my head
not around my heart
strange awareness
grief more intense in my head
memories pictures
objects images
my mind thinking
my small self
focused on loss grief
invisible black bone scarf
not around my heart
my heart experiences
golden love
golden dreams
your golden spirit presence
my heart surrounded by
our golden cocoon
two golden rainbow dragons
our eternal love
my heart embodied soul
bathed in
golden rainbow love
soulmatespiritmates
always forever and beyond
my heart embodied soul

doing better than my head
head focus on loss death
invisible black bone scarf
draped over my shoulders
heart embodied soul
within golden cocoon
our eternal love
peculiar alchemy of grief
hellfires of grief
burning and burning
transforming black into gold
slowly
alchemy of grief
painful slow process
slow transformation
black to gold
alchemy of grief

One Hundred and Sixteen Weeks
January 20, 2014

# Embodied Companions

rereading book bought 1980
yes! bookstore Georgetown
one of our trips together
thinking back over our life
wonderful embodied companions
intense sharing
crucible of love
transformational companions
alchemical crucible
golden cocoon
two as one
wonderful embodied companions
miss my embodied companion
beyond words
so many memories
embodied companions

then everything different
never expected you would
disembody so soon
even though you told me early on
reminded me from time to time
chose not to believe
my mistake
very very sorry
do not know
what else
what more
to say
too late now
to do anything more

than say I am sorry
perhaps tell others
warn others
not to make my mistakes
squander time
pretend embodied life immortal
likely not listen any better than me
will have to live with their own
regrets remorse
like me

treasure our alchemical crucible
golden cocoon
two as one
wonderful embodied companions
miss my embodied companion
beyond words
know I always will

January 20, 2014

# Ultimate Rescue

disembodiment
only fifty seven
**wrong!**
**damn wrong!**
diagnosis December 2009
pancreatic cancer
tumor two years old
survived almost two more years
grateful for those two years
though Carol Susan suffered
cancer surgery
chemo metastasis
more chemo surgery
cancer prevailed
my attempts to rescue
failed miserably
all others attempts
failed miserably too
in the end
Carol Susan
rescued herself
radical rescue
ultimate rescue
disembodiment
Carol Susan's
beautiful radiant spirit
returned to our
spirit realm home
leaving her physical body
no longer a suitable container
for her beautiful radiant spirit

heartbreakingly sad
no miracles
eliminate cancer
restore physical health
no miracles
heartbreakingly sad
Carol Susan
rescued herself
radical rescue
ultimate rescue
disembodiment

January 21, 2014

# Lauren's Procedure

adopted Maya and Merlin's mother Lauren
retiring from mothering kittens
scheduled Lauren's procedure
to make sure
way to procedure
told Lauren
guarantee her retirement
life of leisure
become old cat lady
reminded me of your procedures
told Lauren
you did not stay embodied
become old lady
made me cry
spent yesterday worrying about
Lauren's procedure
remembering yours
sad anxious day
worrying remembering
today Lauren's recovering
lab results good
today not worrying about
Lauren's procedure
monitoring her recovery
remembering your procedures
sad your recovery in spirit realm
radical recovery
ultimate recovery
remembering your procedures
wishing your recovery in physical realm
missing my embodied Kitten

January 24, 2014

# Enough Not Enough

grateful appreciative
for what I had
for what I have
experiences memories
many blessings
grateful appreciative
count my blessings
sometimes blessed with enough
also greedy insatiable
not enough never enough want more

better moments
grateful appreciative   enough
abundance in great measure
blessed with enough

weaker moments
miss my greatest blessing
my embodied companion
appreciation overwhelmed by loss
blessings in the past
not enough never enough want more

best moments
blessed with abundance beyond measure
golden dreams
your golden spirit presence
your soft whisper inspirations
enough more than enough
beyond enough

January 24, 2014

# Lunar New Year Cards 2014

uncertain about sending
Lunar New Year cards
until I realized
Year of the Horse
your Chinese birth year animal
sixty years ago
so decided to send
Lunar New Year cards again
you would be sixty
your next birthday
if still embodied
much rather celebrate
your embodied birthday
than send out
Lunar New Year cards
celebrate both
as best I can

last year sent out
black water snake cards
year before sent out
black water dragon cards
although cards red and gold
this year will send out
green wood horse cards
although cards red and gold
see black horse not green
seems I paint green horse black
although cards red and gold
so I am sending Lunar New Year cards
Lunar New Year 2014
Year of Green Wood Horse
horse still looks black to me

January 24, 2014
Note: "Lunar New Years Cards" (2012) *Hellfires I,* page 79

# Honoring the Dead

*"Then turn to the dead, listen to their lament
and accept them with love."*
C. G. Jung **The Red Book**

listening to the dead
talking to the dead
honoring the dead
the dead are not dead
disembodied from
their physical bodies
why I call them
disembodied
rather than dead
embodied at birth
in the physical realm
disembodied when soul
returns to spirit realm home
disembodied more alive
than embodied
could call the dead
spirits
more true than the dead
listening to the disembodied
talking to the disembodied
honoring the disembodied
disembodied have more wisdom
than embodied
wisdom of angels
wisdom of gods goddesses
wisdom of celestial
golden rainbow dragons
send the disembodied my love

receive their love in return
spirit realm blessings
possession beyond measure
I do more lamenting
than the disembodied
perhaps because
I honor the disembodied
listen to the disembodied
send my love
grateful for inspirations
blessed with golden dreams
other gifts
honoring the disembodied
sending my love
receiving blessings in return
blessings beyond measure
honoring the disembodied

January 26, 2014

Note: quote from
C.G. Jung. *The Red Book: Liber Novus: A Reader's Edition*.
Edited by Sonu Shamdasani. New York: W.W. Norton & Co, 2009,
page 344.

# Heart of Grief

beyond memories
good bad
wonderful horrible
beyond words
good bad
wonderful horrible
beyond images
good bad
wonderful horrible
with good fortune
enter into the
heart of grief
might think
need to find the door
enter a small room
no door
no room
beyond memories
beyond words
beyond images
difficult to describe
heart of grief
with words
drop into heart of hearts
surrounded with golden love
experience heart of grief
I experience heart of grief
now and then
hard to believe sometimes
heart of grief
always here

difficult to be beyond memories
difficult to be beyond words
difficult to be beyond images
enter heart of hearts
experience heart of grief
beyond memories
beyond words
beyond images
experience
pure golden love
always forever and beyond

January 29, 2014

# Lunar New Year 2014

year of the horse
your birth year animal
would be sixty this
year of the horse
if still embodied
year of the green wood horse
horse looks black to me
last year black water snake
year before black water dragon
third lunar new year
since your beautiful radiant spirit
returned to our spirit realm home
expected year of black horse
not green

tradition holds best horses
thirty percent dragon
dragon-horses
superior horses mostly dragon
golden rainbow dragon
surrounding dark green horse
promise of
abundance in great measure
abundance beyond measure

shared black water and cognac with
you and other goddesses
held Chinese coins
burned special incense
ate Chinese food
sent lunar new year cards to

family and friends
sit remembering
better lunar new years
golden lunar new years
embodied together
in our golden cocoon
year of the black wood horse
black horse not green
third worst lunar new year
of my embodied life
blessed we shared many
lunar new years
embodied together
blessed now to share
lunar new year with
golden rainbow dragons
celestial dragons
luminous energy beings

looking with eyes of loss
black dragon 2012
black snake 2013
black horse 2014
looking with eyes of love
spirit vision
golden rainbow dragons
always forever and beyond
blessed with
abundance beyond measure

Lunar New Year 2014
January 31, 2014

Note: "Lunar New Year 2012" *Hellfires I,* page 80
"Lunar New Year 2013" *Hellfires I,* page 230

# "the dead"

do not like the term
"the dead"
do not use the term
"the dead"
totally inaccurate
"the dead"
are not dead
more alive than
embodied people
most embodied people
limited to
physical senses
do not believe in
metasenses
only really alive in dreams
golden dreams of spirit realm
forget most dreams
embodied more dead than
"the dead"
why I use the term
"disembodied"
not "the dead"
term "spirits" even better
spirit realm beings
not "the dead"
call them "the dead"
because do not experience spirits
with physical senses
educated to know better
as in "dead and gone"
"the dead" are disembodied
not gone
changed forms

honoring "the dead"
honoring our loved ones
in their different form
spirit beings
angels
goddesses and gods
not "the dead"
honoring our ancestors
they are not "the dead"
transformed changed forms
spirit realm beings
honoring them with acts of love
nourishes our souls
nourishes our spirit realm
loved ones
they are not "the dead"
if you think so
you have been misinformed
listen to your heart of hearts
your heart of hearts
knows "the dead"
transcended
changed forms
"the dead" are not dead
more alive than "the living"
healing experience
honoring "the dead"

Lunar New Year 2014
January 31, 2014

Note: Written while reading *Lament of the Dead: Psychology after Jung's Red Book* by James Hillman and Sonu Shamdasani, New York: WW Norton & Co, 2013 and *The Red Book: Liber Novus: A Reader's Edition* by C.G. Jung, Edited by Sonu Shamdasani, New York: WW Norton & Co, 2009

# Transcending Dual Realms

abundance in great measure
physical realm
realm of embodied souls
abundance beyond measure
spirit realm
realm of disembodied spirits
physical realm abundance
reduced to memories
since
disembodiment of my soulmate
experience hellfires of grief
woundedness of my heart of hearts
spirit realm abundance
unchanged
no grief
no woundedness
perhaps healing when
two realms
no longer separate
transcending dual realms
transcending polarity
physical realm
realm of the quick
spirit realm
realm of the dead
transcend polarity
in golden dreams
perhaps not transcending
only leave physical realm
behind for a while
know golden dreams healing

do not know about
transcending dual realms
transcending polarities
miss my embodied soulmate
know I always will
experience healing presence
of my disembodied spiritmate
miss physical realm
abundance in great measure
know I always will
blessed with spirit realm
abundance beyond measure
do not know about
transcending polarities
do not know about healing
know golden dreams
visits to spirit realm
with my beloved
healing presence of
eternal love
blessed with golden dreams
presence of my beloved
eternal love

February 2, 2014

# Well of Dreams

mistress of dreams
visits
well of dreams
dips her ladle into
water of dreams
showers dreamer
with
water of dreams

from time to time
mistresses of dreams
meet at well of dreams
share ladle to collect
water of dreams
share water
shower dreamers with
shared ladle
shared water
shared dreams

do not know how many
dream mistresses
there might be
perhaps one per dreamer
do not know

do not understand
nightmares
black water of dreams
perhaps ladle dropped
lower in well of dreams

black stream in
river of dreams
black water
from
well of dreams
perhaps mistress of dreams
wants our attention
make sure do not forget
reminder still have
work to do

experience
golden dreams
golden water from
well of dreams
golden ladle
dream mistress
becomes
goddess of dreams

blessed with
golden dreams

February 3, 2014

Note: My thanks to Denise E. Conner for sharing the image of the
mistress of dreams and for sharing the dream
"Little Bear Mother Bear" **Golden Dreams II,**
January 27, 2014, page 56

# Restoration Miracle

over eight hundred days
indulge in
fantasies of restoration
restoration miracle
before fantasies of healing
healing miracle
no miracles materialize
skills at healing
pitifully meager
skills at restoration
worse

fantasies become dark
your physical remains
ashes in black marble urn
on your shrine
do not possess skills to perform
restoration miracle
become discouraged
heartbroken
filled with despair
failure at healing
failure at restoration

thinking about my restoration fantasies
realize I am able to restore you
any age any time any place
call them memories
not the objective of my fantasies
not restoration miracle
restoration fantasies
tarnished with poison of
logic rational thinking
memory restoration skills

not miracles
provide comfort
paradoxically
remind me of limits of my
restoration skills

no success with physical restoration
drop lower into dragon named grief
concurrently
dragon named grief
drops lower within me
towards center of grief
heart of grief
physical restoration fantasies
tarnished
physical restoration miracle
tarnished
memory restoration
will need to be enough
best I can do
limits of my physical realm skills
wish my restoration fantasies
would come true

miracle of spirit realm experiences
new memories
golden dreams
your golden spirit presence
messages inspirations
infinite compassion
eternal love
beyond physical realm miracles
beyond enough
always forever and beyond

February 6, 2014

# Lost Puppy

remembering your traveling
I wondered around like a lost puppy
while you were gone
waiting for your return
tried to act casual enlightened
about your travels
many chakra cords filaments
connecting us together
we talked every day
when you traveled
still I wondered around like a lost puppy
your absences then luxuries
compared to our current situation
your travel different
heartbreakingly different
soul pain different

intense despair yesterday
aware your subtle spirit presence
feel you rubbing my head
way you used to when embodied
telling me it would be alright
way you used to when embodied
very subtle touch
touched my subtle energy bodies
your golden hands
hands of love
golden love
elegant fingers
comforting your
lost puppy
thank you

February 9, 2014

# Black Water

share black water with
you   other goddesses
each Monday
each month anniversary
other occasions
500 600 700 800 days
birthdays anniversaries holidays
just because sometimes
black water
blood of grief
Kali in Her dark phase
horrible destructive phase
terrible image
strangely satisfying image
sharing black water with
you   other goddesses
black water
blood of grief
will include
other images
eventually
do not know which or when
perseverance patience compassion
discover other images behind
blood of grief
eventually

February 10, 2014

Note: "Grief's Blood Soul's Blood" *Hellfires I,* page 206

# Valentine's Day 2014

third valentine's day
since you disembodied
to become my spirit valentine
thirty four valentines shared embodied
three shared with your new form
miss my embodied valentine
know I always will
even with an angel goddess
spirit valentine
grateful for your subtle presence
golden spirit love
inspirations
put draft cover
DeVaney Wong Workbook
on your shrine
valentine present for us both
shared black water with
you   other goddesses
lit candles incense
wrote in our journal
dream journal too
read "My Spirit Valentine"
from last year
eternal love
eternal valentines
always forever and beyond
my spirit valentine
I love you

February 14, 2014
Note: "My Spirit Valentine" *Hellfires I,* page 235

# Balance

when both embodied
could feel our physical connection
halfway across the world
lonely for your physical presence
never alone
feel our golden cocoon
subtle connections
in my heart of hearts
all energy centers connected
when physically together
connections more intense
golden love
wonderful experiences
wonderful memories

since your disembodiment
miss our intense physical connections
lower physical energy centers
unavailable
subtle bodies energy centers connected
miss our physical realm energy connections
know I always will
even though I experience
subtle spirit realm connections
not as intense for me
my spirit realm perception
unrefined
for some time have felt
my missing your embodied being
as my being flawed
as now and then

experience our spirit realm connection
full force
golden rainbow dragon mother goddess
much more
recognize your energy in any form
soulmatespiritmates

lately realize acceptable to
experience both
missing our embodied connection
grateful for our spirit realm connection
both experiences true
both experiences my reality
hellfires of grief
mixed with
golden dreams
black coexisting with gold
eyes of loss
coexisting with
eyes of love
black gold tai chi
swirling together
multiple realities
healing not transcending loss
healing honoring my loss
missing my embodied companion
honoring our shared physical realm
experiences
memories painful black
mixed with luminous gold
perhaps healing balancing
multiple realities
memories of our shared
embodied experiences

sad no new experiences
shared embodied together
in physical realm
new experiences
hybrid experiences
physical realm spirit realm
mixed
healing treasuring our shared
physical realm experiences
balanced with
treasuring our new experiences
your different form
honoring our shared embodied years
celebrating our shared spirit realm
experiences
accepting my physical realm reality
as best as I can
blended with my spirit realm reality
working towards balance
mixture of memories
experience of love and loss
physical realm
experience of eternal love
spirit realm
always forever and beyond
working towards balance

February 24, 2014

# Balance II

*Hellfires I* two hundred twenty-two
poems
*Golden Dreams I* one hundred eleven
dream poems
*Hellfires II* two hundred twenty-two
poems
*Golden Dreams II* one hundred eleven
dream poems
two to one ratio
ratio not balanced
two black one gold
imbalance
*Hellfires I & II* hints of gold
not balanced
achieve balance requires
patience perseverance compassion
golden dreams
experience subtle spirit realm
visits with my beloved
working towards balance
looking with eyes of love
eyes of my heart of hearts
perhaps balance
one black one gold
do not know
current balance
two black one gold
imbalance
working towards
balance

February 25, 2014

# Horrible Present

horrible present
horrible gift
dragon named grief
swallowed by dragon named grief
swallowed dragon named grief
your disembodiment
most horrible present of my embodied life
struggling with horrible present
twenty eight months
hellfires of grief
black nights of the soul
most horrible present of my embodied life
struggling to transform horrible present
know you others assisting
golden dreams
your subtle spirit presence
eternal golden love
know you others have compassion
for my struggle
appreciate my honoring the dead
transforming horrible present
slowly
very slowly

February 26, 2014

# Twenty Eight Months

twenty eight months ago
you disembodied
twenty eight months ago
returned to our spirit realm home
remembering your disembodiment
twenty eight months ago
cry remembering
all my hearts broken
my heart of heart went with you
your soul no longer embodied
returned to our spirit realm home
remember many sad painful times
before and after your disembodiment
twenty eight months ago
remember many wonderful loving times
at first pretended you were traveling
accurate in a special out of body way
traveled to our spirit realm home
not to return to your physical body
your spirit presence
surrounds me your family others
sitting at your shrine
looking at your pictures
heartbreakingly beautiful
at fifteen eighteen twenty-four fifty
miss your physical presence
treasure our shared memories
treasure your spirit presence
at twenty eight months
burned special incense
lit candles

shared black water
with you   other goddesses
sit at your shrine
crying
remembering
missing
longing
grateful
blessed with golden love
embodied disembodied
blessed with golden dreams
your spirit presence
soulmatespiritmates
always forever and beyond
golden eternal love

Twenty-eight Months
February 28, 2014

# Spirals of Grief

dropping lower
towards center of grief
heart of grief
grief drops lower within
dropping lower in grief
spiraling down lower
within grief
grief within
paradoxical spirals of grief
dropping lower
becoming lighter
rising upward
dropping lower
becoming lighter
not logical
not rational
more real
journeys of my heart
embodied soul
paradoxical spirals of grief
spirals downward  in  heavier  lower
spirals upward  out  lighter  higher
yin yang spirals of grief
coexisting
moving across times
multiple times
past present future
multiple directions
down up vertical
back forth horizontal
multiple levels

multiple realms
physical realms spirit realms
not geometric spirals
chaos spirals
not physical spirals
elemental spirals
earth spirals
fire spirals
water spirals
air spirals
spirit spirals
multiple spirals
chaos spirals
spirals of grief

March 1, 2014

# Pretending

pretending gifts you gave me
never wear out
pretending last forever
gifts of things
some wearing out already
distressing reality
shoes you gave me December 2008
bottoms getting slick
unsafe in wet weather
hoping to replace them with clones
pretend same ones
shoes discontinued
discovery made me cry
pretending gifts never wear out

most important gifts
never wear out
eternal gifts
golden love
golden memories
golden dreams
your golden spirit presence
gifts of soul spirit
never wear out

some gifts wearing out
in spite of my pretending
universe conspiring to help me make space
focus on most important gifts
ones that never wear out

March 4, 2014

# Never Expected

never expected
you to disembody
so soon
compiling DeVaney-Wong Workbook
dream's inspiration
working remembering
many years we planned
working together
DeVaney-Wong International
tell you when I retired
carry your luggage
travel together
be your assistant
studied your materials
read your reference books
never expected
you to disembody
so soon

compiling DeVaney-Wong Workbook
working remembering
never expected
you to disembody
so soon

workbook not luggage
not traveling together
workbook not what I expected
never expected
you to disembody
so soon

March 6, 2014

Note: "Carry Your Luggage" *Hellfires I,*
March 19, 2013, page 265

# DeVaney-Wong Workbook

working on *DeVaney-Wong Workbook*
compiling modules
converting ppt presentations to word
added *The Crone Speaks*
to the appendix
*Fighting Back* too
you started to write
*The Crone Speaks*
June 2009
book length collection
stories of your experiences
consulting facilitations
called them parables
only wrote a few
too ill to continue
year later wrote
*Fighting Back*
presented at Relay For Life
Coral Springs Florida
day after chemotherapy
wishing while working on
**DeVaney-Wong Workbook**
could help you publish
*The Crone Speaks*
instead of
**DeVaney-Wong Workbook**
selfish aspects to my wish
you would still be embodied
in order to finish your book
sorry I cannot do more
**DeVaney-Wong Workbook**

have to be enough
cannot seem to channel
your stories well enough
so *DeVaney-Wong Workbook*
will have to do
wish I could do more
sad you could not finish
*The Crone Speaks*
grow old with me
miss my embodied crone
wishing you were here to speak
struggle to hear
you whispering
from beyond
**DeVaney-Wong Workbook**
best I can do for now
except to tell you
I miss you
send you all my love
best I can do
for now

March 9, 2014

Note: "DeVaney-Wong Workbook," *Golden Dreams II*,
Golden Dream One Hundred Forty-five,
February 10, 2014, page 65

# Three Four

we used to discuss
which was superior
you preferred three
I preferred four
debated merits of each
four square
four elements
three triangle
three essences
body soul spirit
agreed two better
yin yang
female male
agreed one best
tai chi
uroboros
soulmatespiritmates
always forever and beyond

I prefer three now
many reasons why

March 9, 2014

# Lightning of Love

when we first met
I was struck by lightning
fortunately you were too
lightning of love
not only physical realm lightning
lightning of remembering
lightning of connections
across beyond time
past future present
celestial energy
celestial connections
celestial lightning
celestial love
soulmatespiritmates
always forever and beyond

March 11, 2014

Note: Written during inspired work on *DeVaney-Wong Workbook* remembering and experiencing the lightning of love

# Making Room

more aware
enough room for your new form
enough room for your old form
enough room for both
infinite room in my heart

wise advice to make room
for your new form
often focus on your old form
memories of your old form
form now lost
missing
gone

more aware
often focus on loss
your old form
rather than your presence
your new form
creates imbalance

more aware
room for both
infinite room in my heart
infinite room for
love
loss
grief
love
eternal love
infinite room in my heart

beneath my tears
golden love
beneath my loss
your golden presence
beneath my grief
your golden love
beneath my tears
eternal love

more aware
making room means
expanded awareness
infinite room in my heart
working towards balance
love transcends
soulmatespiritmates
always forever and beyond
eternal love

March 13, 2014

Note: "Make Space" *Golden Dreams*, April 26, 2013, page 110

# Doublely Blessed

first blessing
your embodied being
your embodied soul
your spirit presence
your embodied love
first blessing
many blessings
combined

second blessing
your spirit presence
your golden love
your soft whispers
inspirations
memories of first blessing
other memories unfolding
many memories
second blessing
many blessings
combined

grateful for all blessings
soulmatespiritmates
always forever and beyond
eternal love
eternal blessings

March 14, 2014

# Sharing Quintessence

now and then purchase small bag
Godiva chocolate caramel squares
always place one on your shrine
share with you   other goddesses
know you enjoy sharing
quintessence
essence of essence
spirit realm essence
you and other goddesses
do not consume quintessence
experience quintessence
enjoy my sharing
sharing quintessence
with you   other goddesses
enjoy other quintessences
cognac black water
other things
I always eat old chocolate
when I share new
experience physical essence
hint of quintessence
grateful to be
sharing quintessence
with you   other goddesses

March 17, 2014

# Miniature Distillery

long studied alchemy
Christmas 2000
you gave me
miniature distillery
small apparatus
distill wine into brandy
essence of wine
studied miniature distillery
talked about miniature distillery
thought about miniature distillery
never used miniature distillery
treated as decoration

unpacked miniature distillery
at our cottage
thought about wisdom of your gift
adequate energy   too dispersed
adequate fire   too dispersed
focus   too dispersed
intent   too dispersed
wasted opportunity
squandered time

abundance of time now
hellfires of grief
invisible black fire
alchemical fire
internal alchemy
fermentations
calcinations
distillations

works in progress
essences
to be determined

will fire up
miniature distillery
external alchemy
facilitate internal alchemy
as without so within
as within so without
alchemical distillation
slowly refining
distilling essences
alchemical distillation

March 17, 2014

# Alchemy of Longing Love Loss

read about alchemy
studied alchemy
talked about alchemy
words images
processes concepts

experience of
alchemy of longing
waiting discontent
anguish despair
alchemy of longing
knew you would appear
dark haired woman of my dreams
my soulmate

experience of
alchemy of love
intense alchemical fires of love
abundance in great measure
golden cocoon of love
golden crucible of love
magical transformation
alchemy of love
soulmates
two as one
uroboros
physical realm
spirit realm
combined

experience of
alchemy of loss
hellfires of grief
intense invisible black fires
alchemical fires
burn without heat
burn without burning
abundance in great measure
alchemy of loss
alchemy of grief

experience of
alchemy of love
intense alchemical fires of love
abundance beyond measure
golden cocoon of love
golden rainbow dragons
magical transformation
alchemy of love
soulmatespiritmates
always forever and beyond
two as one
uroboros
physical realm
spirit realm
combined
eternal love

March 18, 2014

# Domain Names

today converted ownership
domain names
devaneywong.com .org .net
domain name host
did not blink
coverage expires 2015
your credit card expired
update payment information
maintain ownership
domain names
memorial web site
DeVaney-Wong Workbook
web site
external task easy
painful reminder
your disembodiment
not how we expected
to use
domain names
sad experience
converting ownership
domain names

March 22, 2014

# Ugly Grief Demon

lately dragon named grief
looks more like ugly demon
than dragon
more like ugly temple dog
than dragon
nothing like golden rainbow dragon
ugly temple dog
perhaps ugly temple dog all along
perhaps shape shifter
trickster grief demon
nasty bastard
seems more nasty
than grief dragon
do not like either one
know same
different faces
different look
death    mother of grief demon
death gives birth to grief
dark side of life
life's opposite
death
hell of a shadow
ugly grief demon

March 22, 2014

# Eggs In One Basket

old saying
do not put all your eggs
in one basket
know old saying
disregarded old saying
put all my eggs in one basket
looking back 871 days
post disembodiment
do it again
micro moment
no regrets
putting all my eggs in one basket
basket more subtle now
painfully more subtle
still no regrets
putting all my eggs in one basket
do it again
and again
and again
always forever and beyond

March 22, 2014

# Easy Decision

you would ask me from time to time
if I would do it again
always answered from the heart
yes with no hesitation
easy decision
best decision
looking back 872 days
post disembodiment
if you asked me today
would I make same decision
yes with no hesitation
easy decision
best decision
no regret about decision
always same decision
easy decision
best decision
always forever and beyond

regret your illness
regret your disembodiment
regret not physically present
to ask me again
answer anyway
yes with no hesitation
always same decision
easy decision
best decision
heart of my hearts decision
always forever and beyond

March 23, 2014

Lauren with babies Merlin & Maya
August 26, 2012

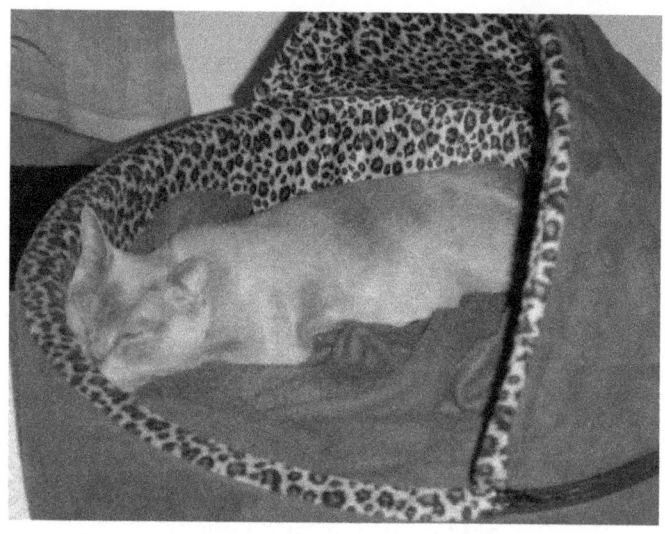

Lauren sleeping February 2014

# All Better

Lauren breathing funny
told her if she laid on my lap
would rub on her
make her all better
told her would not make me
all better
a little better
not all better
made me sad
remembering

will have to be enough
not all better
made me sad
remembering

March 25, 2014

# Curling Up

when half asleep
feel you lying beside me
your head on my shoulder
your arm around me
my arm around you
sometimes my head on your shoulder
when half asleep
as if dreaming
reaching for you
feel my arm around you
your head on my shoulder


waking up
rational thought prevails
attempts to deny
my subtle experiences
no head
no shoulder
no arms
no body
makes me sad
rational thought
limited to physical senses
deny metasenses
subtle energies
your subtle body
your subtle arm around me
your subtle head on my shoulder

enjoy twilight experiences
physical senses half asleep
thinking more diffuse
less rational
experience metasenses
more easily
when half asleep


experience our subtle golden cocoon
your head on my shoulder
wonderful waking dreams
wonderful experiences
curling up
together

March 30, 2014

# Greed

thinking today should be happy
remembering the golden dreams
I remember
I am   except
want to remember more
all golden dreams
greedy to remember
more golden dreams
grateful remembering each golden dream
greedy to remember more
hellfires of grief
not burned up my greed
blessed with golden dreams
abundance beyond measure
greedy for more
all golden dreams
instead more burning in hellfires of grief
long way to go
reduce my greed
wanting all golden dreams
know will eventually experience
all golden dreams
return to our golden spirit realm home
so for now experience
taste glimpse
brief visits to our
golden rainbow spirit realm home
golden dreams

perhaps wanting all golden dreams
not greed after all
heart of my heart's desire
embodied soul's desire
return to our spirit realm home
visit in golden dreams
perhaps rename greed
"sacred desire"
for more golden dreams
all golden dreams
abundance beyond measure
golden dreams
always forever and beyond

March 31, 2014

Note: "All Golden Dreams" *Hellfires II,* December 1, 2013, page 164

# Dreamtime Comfort

comforted one another many years
continue in shared golden dreams
realms overlap in dreamtime
physical realm spirit realm merge
past is present
future is present
present is always forever and beyond
comforting one another
across realms
beyond time
dreamtime shared golden dreams
blessed with golden dreams
dreamtime comfort
always forever and beyond

April 4, 2014

Note: Written after "Comforting Carol Susan"
*Golden Dreams II,* April 3, 2014, page 72

# 888

eight hundred eighty eight days
post disembodiment
your beautiful radiant spirit
returned to our spirit realm home
spark of life left
888 days ago
miss your embodied soul
intensely
not as raw dark despairing
shared golden dreams
soft whispers inspirations
healing golden energy
golden eternal love
today April 8 published
***DeVaney-Wong Workbook***
888 days posthumously
sharing your work
labor of love
honoring you
Workbook CD ready
www.devaneywong.org
your second posthumous web site
sad you could not finish
*The Crone Speaks*
wish you could be here
to finish your book
sad ugly painful reality
DeVaney-Wong Workbook
will have to be enough
sad ugly painful reality

April 8, 2014
888 days

# Salsa

gathering bacon eggs
from refrigerator
making breakfast
saw salsa
remembered how much
you liked to go to breakfast
omelets
western style with salsa
made me sad remembering
not the many times
we shared breakfast
over many years
two embodied souls
sharing breakfast
made me sad remembering
we no longer share
breakfast
in physical realm
left salsa in refrigerator
made me sad
remembering

April 10, 2014

# Naming Things

naming things
provides fantasy of
understanding
control
power
naming things
reduces experience to words
implies
understanding
control
power
naming things
creates illusion of
understanding
control
power
does not work
examples
love
loss
grief
death
no understanding
no control
no power
naming things
better than nothing
not by much

April 10, 2014

# Seasons of Grief

starts with summer
even if you do not realize or
fully appreciate
looking back remember
most always summer

autumn begins
quickly over night for some
slowly over years for others
delicate flowers
wither die
sap flows underground
leaves fall

season of winter
different when grieving
empty    cold
burning   hot
inside
winter of grief
very long season
years not months
different calendar
unrelated to annual seasons
unrelated to outside weather
winter of grief
many years

do not know
spring time of grief
remember spring times
long ago

spring time of grief
sounds like dreaming
spring time in golden dreams
not when awake

know nothing about
summer of grief
unless dreamtime visits
to spirit realm
my beloved
in golden dreams
memory of golden dreams
not when awake

experience autumn of grief
experience winter of grief
memories of past
spring times
summer times
glimpses of spring
glimpses of summer
golden dreams
seasons of grief
unrelated to calendar
not measured in months
measured in years
many years
seasons of grief

April 10, 2014

# A Love Eternal

play "A Love Eternal"
over and over
comforts me in a painful way
reminds me what remains
since your disembodiment
eternal love
blessed with eternal love
possessions beyond measure
miss your physical being
your embodied soul
blessed with memories
love of embodied souls
physical realm experiences of love
miss since your disembodiment
"A Love Eternal"
comforts me in a painful way
comfort of golden dreams
subtle messages
inspirations
sad comfort
physical realm memories
love of two embodied souls
soulmatespiritmates
always forever and beyond

April 12, 2014

Note: My thanks to Peter Sterling for "A Love Eternal"
**Harp Magic**, Harp Magic Music, 1993/2004,
www.harpmagic.com

# Over and Over

sometimes I have the impulse
to write
*I miss you*
over and over
fill up the page
at the bottom write
*I love you always forever and beyond*
fill up page after page
journal after journal
accurate description
of my experience
my reality
resisted the impulse
so far
seems excessive
page after page
over and over
accurate description
of my experience
my reality
resisted the impulse
so far

April 12, 2014

# Dreaming

"I think we dream so we don't have to be apart for so long.
If we're in each other's dreams, we can be together all the time."
A.A. Milne
***Winnie-the-Pooh***

wisdom of A.A. Milne
voice of Winnie-the-Pooh
childlike innocence
wisdom of old soul
lovely expression of soulmates
one function of dreaming
together in dreamtime
always forever and beyond
even if apart in physical realm
glad to remember all dreams
treasure golden dreams
spirit realm dreams
glow with your golden love
golden love of others
why I treasure golden dreams
blessed with golden dreams
dreamtime visits with my beloved
not apart in golden dreams
soulmatespiritmates
always forever and beyond

April 13, 2014

# False Mastery

counting naming
comforting functions
numbers words
against chaos of a
broken heart
impaired metasenses
counting naming
feeble attempts at mastery
no mastery of mysteries
no mastery of spirit realm
pursuing mastery
false goal
numbers words
false mastery
illusion
mastery concept of thinking
logic rationality
glimpses of spirit realm
not mastery
access enough
golden dreams
subtle messages
inspirations
access enough
experience of heart of hearts
embodied soul
abundance beyond measure

April 13, 2014

# Transformation

two embodied soulmates
together
possession in great measure
one soulmate disembodies
one embodied soulmate
remains
embodied soulmate
struggles to remember
spiritmates share eternal love
always forever and beyond
focus on loss
hellfires of grief
black nights of the soul
slow transformation
slowly realize
slowly remember
soulmatespiritmates
combined
physical realm spirit realm
combined
what Carol Susan meant
by making space
transformation
embodied soulmates
to
soulmatespiritmates
not easy transformation
not quick transformation
miss my embodied soulmate
pretended always forever and beyond
eternal love

only true in spirit realm
physical realm embodiment
painfully brief
one embodied soulmate
struggling to transform
soulmates
to
soulmatespiritmates
possession beyond measure
healing transformation
soulmates
to
soulmatespiritmates
always forever and beyond
eternal love

April 16, 2014

Note: "Make Space" *Golden Dreams I,* April 26, 2013, page 110

# Alchemy of the Heart

upper half crucible
spirit realm
lower half crucible
physical realm
sealed together to become
cauldron of the heart
chamber of the spirit
spirit of the heart
heart of hearts
if upper lower crucibles
not locked together
energy leaks escapes
only partial healing occurs
requires balance to seal cauldron
create healing energy within
chamber of the spirit
spirit of the heart
heart of hearts
golden healing energy
alchemy of the heart

April 19, 2014

Note: Written while reading: Eva Wong (translator). ***Harmonizing Yin and Yang: The Dragon-Tiger Classic***. Boston: Shambhala, 1997

# Easter 2014

third Easter since your disembodiment
your beautiful radiant spirit
returned to our spirit realm home
Easter 2011 your last Easter embodied
we used to celebrate Easter
now observe Easter
no celebration

embodied you were the Easter Bunny
of our small family
miss my embodied Easter Bunny
we used to celebrate Easter
now observe Easter
no celebration
third Easter since
my Easter Bunny disembodied
miss my embodied Easter Bunny
always my Easter Bunny
spirit Easter Bunny
I love you
always forever and beyond

April 20, 2014
Easter Sunday
900 days

Note: "Easter 2012" *Hellfires I,* April 8, 2012, page 102

# 900 Days

900 days
Easter Sunday
your soul no longer embodied
third Easter
another sad holiday
no longer share with you
in your physical body
share with your subtle spirit presence
not the same somehow
your physical presence missing
physical body energy connections missing
lower chakra connections missing
used to feel missing your physical presence
being ungrateful unappreciative
of your subtle spirit presence
awareness of missing physical energy connections
enabled me to realize both true
both reality of my experience
paradoxically contradictory
both true authentically true
miss your physical presence
shared physical connections
physical realm energy
grateful appreciative for your
subtle spirit presence
abundance beyond measure
Easter Sunday
900 days

April 20, 2014
Easter Sunday
900 Days

# I Remember

hearing about someone
lost their companion of many years
made me very sad made me cry
remembering
crying telling you
I remember
over and over
holding you just before
you disembodied
helping you lie down
take your last few breaths
your beautiful radiant spirit
returning to our spirit realm home
made me very sad remembering
made me cry
experience seemed so fresh
felt like only yesterday
or this afternoon
painful experience
painful memory
heartbreakingly sad
remembering through my tears
felt like only yesterday
or this afternoon
burned extra incense
honoring the couple
honoring you and me
remembering
always

April 22, 2014

# Black Lead of Grief

with loss
heart becomes black lead
heavy
dark
raw
experience black hellfires of grief
hellfires burn without burning
alchemical fire in heart of hearts
embodied soul's domain
hellfires of grief
alchemical fire
slowly transforms
black lead of loss grief
glimpses of silver gold
memories
golden dreams
subtle whispers
inspirations
spirit presence
eternal love

April 26, 2014

# Half A Heart

two embodied hearts become one
two embodied souls become one
two become one
one heart disembodies
one soul disembodies
one embodied heart becomes one half
one embodied soul becomes one half
half a heart
half a soul
true and not true
paradox of two become one
paradox of one becomes one half
half a heart
half a soul
true in physical realm
not true in physical realm
paradox of truth
other half a heart invisible
other half a soul invisible
too subtle for physical senses
embodied soul knows
heart of hearts knows
two hearts are one
two souls are one
soulmatespiritmates
always forever and beyond

April 28, 2014

# Some Days

some days are
worse than others
today is one
dark heavy raw
nothing helps
crying perhaps a little
took a nap
wrote
nothing helps
crying perhaps a little
played with Lauren
Lauren helps a little too

two and one half years
here soon
your 60$^{th}$ birthday
if still embodied
soon after
mothers day
soon after
three in a row
two used to be celebrations
all sad days now

some days are
worse than others
today is one
nothing helps
crying perhaps a little
Lauren helps a little too

April 29, 2014

# Embodied Companion

do not like
being without
my embodied companion
enough to say
for now

April 29, 2014

# Photographs

our photographs
glad we have them
wish we had more
help activate memories
help activate feelings
return to time
photographs were taken
re-experience over and over
wish we were making more
camera does not work
in spirit realm
depend on my dream vision
waking memories of dreamtime
visits to spirit realm
glad we have photographs
wish we had more
glad for new memories
spirit realm visits in my dreams
reduced to word pictures
in dream journals
dream poems
pictures of spirit realm
stored in my heart of hearts
blessed with golden dreams
abundance beyond measure

April 29, 2014

# Thirty Months

thirty black months
two and a half black years
since your beautiful radiant spirit
returned to our spirit realm home
worst thirty months of my life
invisible black hellfires of grief
black nights of the soul
thirty hard months
miss your loving physical presence
grateful for golden dreams
your loving spirit presence
loving spirit presence of
Carlos Eldon and ancestors
subtle whispers inspirations
golden rainbow dragons

black darker at thirty months
missing more raw intense
blackness of loss heavier
miss my embodied companion
worst thirty months of my life
struggle towards equilibrium
fall short
special days hardest
darkest rawest heaviest
thirty months
doing best I can
have to be good enough
thirty months
hellfires of grief intense

know I am to make space for
spirit realm Carol Susan
at thirty months
mostly looking back
space crowded with memories
physical realm Carol Susan

now special days have
different kind of abundance
sorry I am not doing better
making space
abundance of memories
at first all black
sometimes see golden center
blessed with
warm loving memories
warm loving experiences
miss making more
with my embodied companion
special days difficult time
to make space
new experiences
new memories
with my disembodied companion
sorry I am not doing
better making space
doing best I can
special days more difficult
not rational not logical
do not care
doing best I can
good enough
no blame

thirty months different from
eighteen months
twenty four months
more crude less detached
closer to core
words more difficult
closer to raw experience
difficult translating
soul's tears into words
words not needed near core
words not available near core
tears healing without words
very slow painful
transformation
with or without words
with or without awareness
with or without external tears
essence of embodied soul's tears
contained in physical tears
slow alchemical process
years and more years
worst thirty months of my life
doing the best I can
good enough
no blame

April 30, 2014

Note: "Eighteen Months" *Hellfires I,* page 299
"Eighteen Months II, **Hellfires I,** page 309
"Disembodiment Day, Year Two" (twenty four months)
*Hellfires II*, page 132

# All My Heart

realize half a heart
inaccurate
when we met
gave you
all my heart
not half a heart
all my heart
blessed with abundance
beyond measure
you gave me yours
heart of our hearts
shared hearts
one heart
two hearts become one
one heart
in sacred chamber of
my heart of hearts
your heart lives within mine
mine lives within yours
soulmates spiritmates
soulmatespiritmates
always forever and beyond
blessed with
abundance beyond measure

May Day/Beltane
May 1, 2014

Note: "Half A Heart" **Hellfires II,** April 28, 2014, page 277

# Soror Mystica

soror mystica
usually translated
mystic sister
so much more
yin and yang
earth and sky
sun and moon
male and female
queen and king
husband and wife
companions
partners
soul mates
spirit mates
soulmatespiritmates
my embodied soul mate
my soror mystica
disembodied
my soror mystica
now subtle companion
always my soror mystica
across beyond time
different names
different faces
different bodies
same soul
always my soror mystica
soulmatespiritmates
always forever and beyond

Beltane
May 1, 2014

First Meeting Lauren & Eldon
October 2012

Lauren & incense August 2014

# Pregnant With Death

pregnant with death
since my soulmate
got sick   disembodied
all pregnant with death
many pretend otherwise
undiscovered for some
does not show
death hovers inside
grows large
larger
with loss of loved ones
largest
with disembodiment of soulmate
many avert their eyes
attempt to deny
embodied soul knows
all pregnant with death
part of physical realm life
do not ask me why
do not know
do not like
being pregnant with death
anymore than you
wonder what
birth from death
looks like
already know
experiences glimpses in golden dreams
wonderful visits to celestial realm
with my beloved
grateful for golden dreams
blessed with golden dreams

May 7, 2014

Note: Wrote after reading Irvin D. Yalom, **Staring at the Sun: Overcoming the Terror of Death.** SanFrancisco: Jossey-Bass: 2009

# Carol Susan's Birthday 2014

sixty years old today
if embodied
third birthday
since you disembodied
shared thirty-three birthdays
embodied together
happy celebrations
miss your physical being intensely
more intensely on special days
your sixtieth birthday
if embodied
Year of Green Wood Horse
your birth year animal
horse looks mostly black
perhaps a little green
with golden glow
now and then horse becomes
golden rainbow dragon

for your sixtieth birthday
two presents on your shrine
**DeVaney-Wong Workbook**
**DeVaney-Wong Workbook CD**
few other things
ate Chinese food
shared black water   cognac
with you   other goddesses
burned extra incense
one for each year

celebrated three birthdays
since you disembodied
as best we can
sit at your shrine
remembering your birthdays
many other memories
crying
celebrating your sixtieth birthday
as best as I can
your birthday always
day of celebration
know you are present
remembering with us
celebrating with us
aware of your
golden rainbow dragon
mother goddess energy
grateful we are together
in whatever form
sharing birthdays together

May 8, 2014

Note: "Carol Susan's Birthday 2012" *Hellfires I,* page 110
"Carol Susan's Birthday 2013" *Hellfires II,* page 2

60+ incense

# Mothers Day 2014

we celebrated Mothering Ones Day
many years both embodied
not enough years
birth of our daughter
added Mothers Day
combined them
two into one
golden rainbow dragon mother
golden rainbow dragon mothering one
Mothers Day 2014
third since you disembodied
miss my embodied mothering one
every day
know I always will
exceptional mothering one
still my mothering one
different form
spirit mothering one
blessed with my
exceptional mothering one

May 11, 2014

Note: "Mothering Ones Day 2013" *Hellfires II,* page xx
"Mothers Day 2012" *Hellfires I,* page 114

# Return

returned to our cottage
away twenty three months
returned with our daughter
her new PhD
Lauren Maya Merlin
our daughter
Maya Merlin
will move soon
new academic job
sitting in your shrine room
in our cottage
fifty pictures
images of you
images of us
early pictures
wedding pictures
anniversary pictures
last embodied birthday
last embodied Christmas
our daughter's birthday
last one three of us shared
embodied
wall of last pictures
intense experience
our shrine room
sad comfort seeing walls of pictures
remembering happier times
placed new purple orchid
at your shrine
sit at your shrine
each day remembering

thirty one months yesterday
not unpacked traveling shrine
only your black marble urn
enough for now
burn incense
light candles
sit at your shrine
remembering
times embodied together
golden dreams
inspirations
best I can do for now
does not seem like enough
returned to our cottage
placed your black marble urn
on your shrine
cottage not same
since your disembodiment
thirty one months ago
nothing the same
since you disembodied
return to our cottage
cottage lost its charm
thirty one months ago
except for memories
only fifty pictures
in your shrine room
infinite number in my
heart of hearts
life times
always forever and beyond

June 1, 2014

# Cottage's Energy

our cottage charged with
intense energy
everything I touch
with my eyes   hands
years of memories
not residual energy
more intense
our combined energies
energy of ancestors
our daughter
returning to cottage
after almost two years
experience intense energy
so many memories
overwhelming
comforting
distressing
blended together
relive experiences
so many memories
intense energy
intense love
blessed with memories
struggle with intense energy
mixture of love loss sadness
after two years away
struggle to balance
cottage's energy
reality of my experience
glad to experience
such intense energy

so many memories
sorry not making
more room for
new subtle experiences
overwhelmed with
cottage's energy
enough for now
more than enough
beyond enough

June 12, 2014

# True Shrine

reestablished your shrine
at our cottage
some items below
in drawers
once held other things
now contain memories
seven candles
light only one
Lauren curious about fire
images of goddesses
others invisible
still present
purple orchid
your favorite pictures
my favorite pictures
black linen cloth
made for your shrine
physical shrine
comforting
sadly comforting
sad need a shrine
shrine sadly comforting
not enough room
at physical shrine
infinite room in
my heart of hearts
your true shrine

June 17, 2014

# Invisible

sun light flooded
your shrine
your picture
your purple orchid
little Lauren sit looking
watching sunbeam
illuminating your shrine
told her
you are invisible
she looked at me
as if to say
you do not know
how to see
silly to think
you are invisible
Lauren can see
much better
than me
new teacher

June 30, 2014

# Empty Nest

our daughter
her two cats
moved
new job
new area
cottage now
empty nest
always imagined
share empty nest
with you
mother bird
father bird
together
our cottage
our little nest
never imagined
share cottage
with
spirit mother bird
and
little gray cat
embodied mother bird
left our nest
970 days ago
always imagined
share empty nest
with you
different form
than I imagined
miss sharing
empty nest

with my
embodied mother bird
sharing empty nest
with
spirit mother bird
and
little gray cat
reality of my experience
making the best of it
not easy
your half of our little nest
often seems empty
when looking with
eyes of loss
when looking with
eyes of love
experience
spirit form
mother bird

June 30, 2014

# Despair II

looking at one of our last pictures
embodied together
you were very sick in such pain
I look more anguished
you were fully present
making the best of each moment
quiet courage
while I was experiencing such despair
in anticipation
you embracing each moment
I struggling with despair
anticipating loss of my embodied soulmate
I am sorry I was not more courageous
graceful embracing the moment like you
you dying to your physical body
embracing life
while I was embracing despair
loss grief death
you dying to your physical body
much more alive than me
while I was drowning in despair
your were fully present
making the most of each moment
I am sorry I could do no better
already looking with eyes of loss
you always looked from eyes of love
your disembodiment process no exception
quiet dignity
971 days post disembodiment
filled with despair
could not replicate

your quiet courage then
still can not
no longer anticipating loss
loss 971 days real
looking at our picture
soulmates holding one another
seems so very long ago
look at our embrace with
such intense longing
intense loss
then feel intense love
remembering our holding one another
hand in hand
looking into the void together
you more graceful than me
still not graceful
miss you too much
too much loss
too much raw grief
loneliness
most of the time
realize you will not return
in your embodied form
still dream
fantasize
know false hope
does no harm to dream
fantasize
ugly woundedness of
your disembodiment
sinking in
deeper
lower
almost 1000 days

picture seems so very long ago
embracing one another
hand in hand
embodied
together
looking into the void
together
blessed with memories
images
inspirations
golden dreams

Note: *"Despair"* **Hellfires II**, October 6, 2013, page 117

July 1, 2014

2011

# A Few Moments

we shared more than
a few moments
we shared many moments
remembering the many moments
do not make me cry
remembering when the moments
turned dark
then black
make me cry
miss sharing new moments
with my embodied soulmate
moments stopped
when you disembodied
moments of loss prevail
missing your physical presence
struggling to make room for
your spirit presence
golden rainbow energy
surrounding me with love
new kind of sharing
more than
a few moments
new kind of sharing
miss other kind of sharing
know I always will

July 17, 2014

# Dreams Underground

dreams underground
despair too intense to remember
experience enough despair
without dreams of despair
dreams hiding underground
holding golden dreams hostage
adds to despair
golden dreams underground too
reality of my experience
approaching 1000 days
36 wedding anniversary
33 months
dreams too intense
to remember
hiding underground
compassionate act of kindness
miss remembering golden dreams
blessed beyond measure
with golden dreams
even the ones
I do not remember

July 23, 2014

# 999

nine hundred ninety nine
days
999 days
since your embodied soul
disembodied
returned to our spirit realm home
999 days
black days
raw days
hard days
999
only a number
yet significant in
indefinable way
endured 999 days
hellfires of grief
black nights of the soul
no grace to my endurance
raw awful black grief
keeping track of days
may seem excessive
embodied soul
endures loss of soulmate
count days weeks months years
999 days
experience hellfires of grief
999 days
and
counting

July 29, 2014

# 1000 and 36

36 wedding anniversary
today
third in your new form
1000 days in your new form
today
I miss celebrating
sharing our anniversaries
with your old form
now observe our anniversaries
blessed we shared
33 wedding anniversaries
embodied together
heartbroken we did not
share more anniversaries
embodied together
heartbroken we did not
grow old
embodied together

planted large ginkgo tree
back yard of our cottage
named the tree 1000 and 36
1000 days
today
36 wedding anniversary
today
1036 tree
few leaves fell during planting
placed them at your shrine
will add golden ginkgo leaves
in the fall

shared black water
cognac
quiet day
sad day
no celebrations
no special food
hellfires of grief
1000 days
black nights of the soul
1000 days

July 30, 2014

Note: *34<sup>th</sup> Wedding Anniversary,* **Hellfires I,** page 116
*35<sup>th</sup> Wedding Anniversary,* **Hellfires II**, page 60

# Blessed

blessed with golden dreams
presence of my beloved
soulmatespiritmate
abundance beyond measure
always forever and beyond
eternal love

August 5, 2014

Note: *Blessed With Golden Dreams*, **Hellfires II,**
September 14, 2013, page 98

# Alone II

never felt alone
when you were embodied
no matter where in the world
you were
never felt alone
now I feel alone
know not true
alone when looking
from eyes of loss
not alone when looking
from eyes of love
your physical body
gone
your energy
remains
your spirit presence
remains
your subtle whispers
remain
could call them inspirations
messages from my muse
visit you in golden dreams
feel your golden love
always forever and beyond
eternal love
know I am not alone
sometimes use
the wrong eyes

August 6, 2014

Note: *Alone,* **Golden Dreams I,** Dream Eighty-five,
July 12, 2013, page 135

# Disbelief

there are times
I do not believe
you disembodied
in spite
of the evidence
I understand my disbelief
I do not want to believe
pretend otherwise
used to scold myself
when I caught myself
indulging in disbelief
now more compassionate
your disembodiment
very slow process for me
cushioned by disbelief
there are often times
I do not believe
you disembodied
in spite
of the evidence
paradox of disbelief
know you disembodied
do not believe
you disembodied
do not want to believe
so I pretend
often catch myself pretending
indulging in disbelief
might suspect
disbelief provides
protective function

does not
really
work
your disembodiment
very long painful process for me
your disembodiment
happened between
your last breath
and
absence of the next
moment continues
for me
disbelief
helps
a little
sometimes
but not very much
if at all

August 6, 2014

1000 & 36 ginkgo tree

# Projects

invent projects
to attempt respite
from
hellfires of grief
temporary relief
hellfires not diminished
by projects
when project completed
hellfires return
with increased energy
temporary relief
at best

August 6, 2014

# Wolves of Despair

images of wolves of despair
not at the door
not inside the house
inside my heart
wolves of despair
seem to exist on
loss
heartache
loneliness
drinking tears
diet of grief
perhaps I have only
animated hellfires of grief
perhaps wolves of despair
been here all along
only now recognize their shapes
hellfires' wolves
occurred to me
need to learn
their names
next occurred to me
already know
impossible to pronounce
impossible to say
impossible to convert images
into words
know wolves of despair
taken up residence
in my heart
few experiences demystify
wolves of despair

golden dreams
presence of golden rainbow dragon
few others   unnamed
wolves of despair
will not go hungry
wolves of despair
know them
all too well

August 9, 2014

# Pink Disposable Razors

green razor dull
looked for new one
bag empty
found another bag
pink disposable razors
laying in cabinet
almost three years
perhaps longer
you no longer need
pink disposable razors
compared pink with green
almost the same
now using
pink disposable razors
know you would smile
in your corporal form
waste not want not
sense you smiling
every time I use
pink disposal razors

August 9, 2014

# Pink Disposable Razors II

all except the one
you last used
still in our shower
almost three years
holds some of your energy
too much to relocate
much less throw away
voice says
can't keep everything
do not know why not
enough room
does no harm
no blame
offers small comfort
holds some of your energy
may eventually place
pink disposable razor
at expanded shrine
fine where it is
for now

August 9, 2014

# NO!

NO! NO! NO! NO! NO! NO! NO! NO! NO! NO! NO!
NO! NO! NO! NO! NO! NO! NO! NO! NO! NO! NO!
NO! NO! NO! NO! NO! NO! NO! NO! NO! NO! NO!
NO! NO! NO! NO! NO! NO! NO! NO! NO! NO! NO!
NO! NO! NO! NO! NO! NO! NO! NO! NO! NO! NO!
NO! NO! NO! NO! NO! NO! NO! NO! NO! NO! NO!
NO! NO! NO! NO! NO! NO! NO! NO! NO! NO! NO!
NO! NO! NO! NO! NO! NO! NO! NO! NO! NO! NO!
NO! NO! NO! NO! NO! NO! NO! NO! NO! NO! NO!
NO! NO! NO! NO! NO! NO! NO! NO! NO! NO! NO!
NO! NO! NO! NO! NO! NO! NO! NO! NO! NO! NO!
NO! NO! NO! NO! NO! NO! NO! NO! NO! NO! NO!
NO! NO! NO! NO! NO! NO! NO! NO! NO! NO! NO!
NO! NO! NO! NO! NO! NO! NO! NO! NO! NO! NO!
NO! NO! NO! NO! NO! NO! NO! NO! NO! NO! NO!
NO! NO! NO! NO! NO! NO! NO! NO! NO! NO! NO!
NO! NO! NO! NO! NO! NO! NO! NO! NO! NO! NO!
NO! NO! NO! NO! NO! NO! NO! NO! NO! NO! NO!
NO! NO! NO! NO! NO! NO! NO! NO! NO! NO! NO!
NO! NO! NO! NO! NO! NO! NO! NO! NO! NO! NO!
NO! NO! NO! NO! NO! NO! NO! NO! NO! NO! NO!
NO! NO! NO! NO! NO! NO! NO! NO! NO! NO! NO!
NO! NO! NO! NO! NO! NO! NO! NO! NO! NO! NO!
NO! NO! NO! NO! NO! NO! NO! NO! NO! NO! NO!
NO! NO! NO! NO! NO! NO! NO! NO! NO! NO! NO!
NO! NO! NO! NO! NO! NO! NO! NO! NO! NO! NO!
NO! NO! NO! NO! NO! NO! NO! NO! NO! NO! NO!
NO! NO! NO! NO! NO! NO! NO! NO! NO! NO! NO!

August 10, 2014

# WHY?

WHY? WHY? WHY? WHY? WHY? WHY? WHY?
WHY? WHY? WHY? WHY? WHY? WHY? WHY?
WHY? WHY? WHY? WHY? WHY? WHY? WHY?
WHY? WHY? WHY? WHY? WHY? WHY? WHY?
WHY? WHY? WHY? WHY? WHY? WHY? WHY?
WHY? WHY? WHY? WHY? WHY? WHY? WHY?
WHY? WHY? WHY? WHY? WHY? WHY? WHY?
WHY? WHY? WHY? WHY? WHY? WHY? WHY?
WHY? WHY? WHY? WHY? WHY? WHY? WHY?
WHY? WHY? WHY? WHY? WHY? WHY? WHY?
WHY? WHY? WHY? WHY? WHY? WHY? WHY?
WHY? WHY? WHY? WHY? WHY? WHY? WHY?
WHY? WHY? WHY? WHY? WHY? WHY? WHY?
WHY? WHY? WHY? WHY? WHY? WHY? WHY?
WHY? WHY? WHY? WHY? WHY? WHY? WHY?
WHY? WHY? WHY? WHY? WHY? WHY? WHY?
WHY? WHY? WHY? WHY? WHY? WHY? WHY?
WHY? WHY? WHY? WHY? WHY? WHY? WHY?
WHY? WHY? WHY? WHY? WHY? WHY? WHY?
WHY? WHY? WHY? WHY? WHY? WHY? WHY?
WHY? WHY? WHY? WHY? WHY? WHY? WHY?
WHY? WHY? WHY? WHY? WHY? WHY? WHY?
WHY? WHY? WHY? WHY? WHY? WHY? WHY?
WHY? WHY? WHY? WHY? WHY? WHY? WHY?
WHY? WHY? WHY? WHY? WHY? WHY? WHY?
WHY? WHY? WHY? WHY? WHY? WHY? WHY?
WHY? WHY? WHY? WHY? WHY? WHY? WHY?
WHY? WHY? WHY? WHY? WHY? WHY? WHY?

August 10, 2014

# DAMN!

DAMN! DAMN! DAMN! DAMN! DAMN! DAMN!
DAMN! DAMN! DAMN! DAMN! DAMN! DAMN!
DAMN! DAMN! DAMN! DAMN! DAMN! DAMN!
DAMN! DAMN! DAMN! DAMN! DAMN! DAMN!
DAMN! DAMN! DAMN! DAMN! DAMN! DAMN!
DAMN! DAMN! DAMN! DAMN! DAMN! DAMN!
DAMN! DAMN! DAMN! DAMN! DAMN! DAMN!
DAMN! DAMN! DAMN! DAMN! DAMN! DAMN!
DAMN! DAMN! DAMN! DAMN! DAMN! DAMN!
DAMN! DAMN! DAMN! DAMN! DAMN! DAMN!
DAMN! DAMN! DAMN! DAMN! DAMN! DAMN!
DAMN! DAMN! DAMN! DAMN! DAMN! DAMN!
DAMN! DAMN! DAMN! DAMN! DAMN! DAMN!
DAMN! DAMN! DAMN! DAMN! DAMN! DAMN!
DAMN! DAMN! DAMN! DAMN! DAMN! DAMN!
DAMN! DAMN! DAMN! DAMN! DAMN! DAMN!
DAMN! DAMN! DAMN! DAMN! DAMN! DAMN!
DAMN! DAMN! DAMN! DAMN! DAMN! DAMN!
DAMN! DAMN! DAMN! DAMN! DAMN! DAMN!
DAMN! DAMN! DAMN! DAMN! DAMN! DAMN!
DAMN! DAMN! DAMN! DAMN! DAMN! DAMN!
DAMN! DAMN! DAMN! DAMN! DAMN! DAMN!
DAMN! DAMN! DAMN! DAMN! DAMN! DAMN!
DAMN! DAMN! DAMN! DAMN! DAMN! DAMN!
DAMN! DAMN! DAMN! DAMN! DAMN! DAMN!
DAMN! DAMN! DAMN! DAMN! DAMN! DAMN!
DAMN! DAMN! DAMN! DAMN! DAMN! DAMN!
DAMN! DAMN! DAMN! DAMN! DAMN! DAMN!

August 10, 2014

# NO! WHY? DAMN!

easy to write
painful to experience
live every day
over and over
DAMN! no answer to WHY?
best I can do
NO! spoken from the heart
WHY? embodied soul's lament
DAMN! heart of hearts' lament
best I can do for now
will have to be enough
like dreams
words underground
only few words remain
perhaps only a few needed
no lack of memories
no lack of images
no lack of love
no lack of grief
no lack of hellfires
NO! WHY? DAMN!
best I can do for now
will have to be enough

August 11, 2014

east: day side

west: night side

August 13, 2014

# Tai Chi Flag

made tai chi flag
yin purple yang lavender
background black
flag outside cottage
over two years
east side sun side
day side
faded
damaged torn holes
nylon dissolving
purple now lavender
lavender almost white
black now gray
reflects my daytime experience
hellfires of grief
western side moon side
night side
like new
no damage
reflects my nighttime experience
golden dreams
two modes of experience
hellfires of day
golden dreams of night
why I prefer night
thinking I should replace
tai chi flag
day side looks tattered
night side like new
reflects my two modes of experience
decided to leave it up a little longer

August 13, 2014

# Sharing Lychees

got fresh lychees at Asian market
sit at our table eating fresh Lychees
remembering
how we used to share lychees
when both embodied
dried lychees
fresh lychees
lychee ice cream
eating fresh lychees
placed one at your shrine
remembering
sharing lychees
when both embodied
we continue sharing lychees
different now
you enjoy essence of lychees
leave physical lychees for me
much prefer our old way of
sharing lychees
old way no longer available
sharing lychees
our new way
makes me cry

August 14, 2014

# Beach Condo 1977

went to beach 2014
rented ocean front condo
third floor
reminded me a little
of our ocean front condo
fourth floor
where we lived in 1977
sweet bitter sweet memories
bitter only because
you are not physically present
to reminisce with me
mostly sweet sweet memories
when we found one another
rediscovered our golden cocoon
golden rainbow cocoon
intense love
intense energy
soulmates
when we first met
souls already knew
so very happy to be reunited
once again
difficult being sad
about our beginnings
this embodied lifetime
such power magic mystery
blessed to find my soulmate
blessed with golden memories
beach condo 1977

August 19, 2014

# Beach Condo Recreated

setting at beach
remembering our beach condo
fantasize buying unit
like our beach condo
where we lived in 1977
perhaps same unit
at least same building
realize would not be the same
could recreate most everything
except my embodied soulmate
would be missing
fantasy spoiled
be an old man
alone at the beach with
memories of 1977
know cannot recreate
beach condo 1977
do not really need to
1977 lives in my heart of hearts
always forever and beyond

August 19, 2014

# Dirty Navel

putting arnica on my sunburn
noticed red scar below my navel
then noticed my dirty navel
remembered how you
would announce
your navel is dirty
proceed to collect q-tips baby oil
attack my dirty navel
warm loving memories
now no q-tips no baby oil
no embodied soul mate
to tidy up my dirty navel
golden memories
wonderful experiences
blessed for the many years
you tidied up my dirty navel
blessed with experiencing
your loving
caring ways
heartbroken you are no longer
physically present
to tidy up my
dirty navel

August 19, 2014

# My Birthday 2014

third birthday since
your beautiful radiant spirit
returned to our spirit realm home
miss your embodied presence
every day
seems more intense
on special days
blessed we shared
thirty four birthdays
embodied together
last three birthdays
shared with
your spirit presence
miss your physical presence
blessed with your spirit presence
golden dreams
inspirations
other things
birthdays not the same
since your disembodiment
now spend birthdays
remembering
other birthdays
celebrated
embodied together

August 20, 2014

# Inadequate Words

inadequate words
unable to communicate
intensity
depth
grief
loss
longing
repeat myself
over and over
best I can
inadequate words
do not deter
struggle to find words
describe my experiences
best I can
necessary even with
inadequate words

August 22, 2014

# Mysteries

thrown into heart of mysteries
disembodiment of my beloved
swirling black chaos
hellfires of grief
loss
longing
mysteries
death
life
birth
now and again
veil fades
beyond swirling blackness
spirit realm
greatest of mysteries
eternal love

August 25, 2014

# Dreaming II

waking up
with tears in my eyes
know dreaming
about your disembodiment
even though do not
remember the dream
experience of
waking up
with tears in my eyes
more than enough
thought re-experience
your disembodiment
awake often enough
perhaps not
waking up
with tears in my eyes

September 3, 2014

Note: *Dreaming,* **Hellfires II**, April 13, 2014, page 268

# Things

things are only important
because we share them
things hold memories of
our sharing
our togetherness
our energy
each holds
a tiny bit of
our love

otherwise things
are
only things

September 8, 2014

# Presences

returned to our cottage
away twenty four days
little Lauren looking about
told her our cottage
filled with presences
only two corporeal bodies
many spirit presences
strongest presence my beloved
told little Lauren
could not see you
with physical realm eyes
could feel you
not with fingers or hands
within my heart of hearts
your presence very strong
your loving energy
know little Lauren
can see presences
better than me
unsure she understood
my explanations
she does not need to understand
she knows beyond understanding
not separate realities for her
she listened politely
seemed pleased with my progress
perceiving presences

September 8, 2014

# Sadness Attacks

my heart aches always
though at times
sadness attacks
with
intense fierceness
sadness
missing
longing
old companions
more intense
nearing third anniversary
of your disembodiment
eyes of loss
dominate
eyes of love
over shadowed by
intense attacks
sadness
missing
longing
eyes of love experience
eternal love
blessed with eternal love

September 13, 2014

# Halloween 1977

Halloween 1977
our first together
got you a pumpkin
your first
picture of you
holding your pumpkin
one of my favorites
you were so very happy
holding your pumpkin
still experience your joy
looking at your picture
on wall of memories
Halloween 2010
first in our cottage
last Halloween both embodied
Halloween 2011 Disembodiment Day
no longer celebrate Halloween
no longer observe Halloween
observe Disembodiment Day
Halloween no longer exists
October 31$^{st}$ will always be
Disembodiment Day
as long as I am embodied
Disembodiment Day Year Three
month and a half away
blessed with other memories
better memories
golden memories
golden dreams
your spirit presence
inspirations
blessed with eternal love

September 14, 2014

# Eternal Love

eternal love
connections
flowing
backwards forwards
timelessness of eternity
surrounded permeated
inside and out with
eternal love
outside time
beyond time
always forever and beyond
blessed with
eternal love

September 15, 2014

# Simple Pleasures

watching Lauren
playing with
her mouse string toy
totally focused
full of joy
playing with her mouse
her joy contagious
travels up the string
experiencing simple pleasures
playing with Lauren
and her mouse

September 15, 2014

2009

2010

# Physical Touch

memory wall pictures
you holding me
physical holding
physical touch
now experience
your subtle spirit touch
miss your physical touch
more than I
know how to say
blessed with your
physical touch
blessed with your
spirit touch
long for your physical touch
spoiled by your loving ways
blessed with your
spirit touch
eternal love
miss your physical touch
beyond words

September 15, 2014

# Heavy Hearts

autumn equinox
transition summer to fall
in eight days be
thirty five months
thirty one days later
disembodiment day
year three
thinking about transitions
experiencing heavy hearts
heavy with transitions
memories of other autumns
driving in mountains
walking in leaves
with you
aware of my blessings
count them everyday
thankful for my blessings
heart heavy with
memories
longing
missing
overflowing with love
thankful for my heavy heart
broken by loss
yet full of love
image of you
Carlos Eldon
and others
holding my broken hearts
together
with golden hands

energy hands
energy beings
healing my broken hearts
heart seemed lighter before
numb with grief
now heavy full
experience transitions with
eyes of love
heavy heart
full of sadness
missing
longing
and
love
eternal love
blessed with eternal love
thank you

September 22, 2014
Autumn Equinox

# Poquito Energy

since your disembodiment
most of your things
remain in place
approaching three years
think perhaps time
to do something with
your physical realm things
make more space
for your spirit presence
aware each of
your physical realm things
retains your energy
slightest amount
poquito energy
things you used wore cherished
each retains bit of your energy
poquito energies of your things
generate memories
golden times
dark times
black times
disposed sick room things
your black marble urn
your physical remains
constant reminder of black times
more than enough energy
intense memories
black times
find comfort in
poquito energy of your things
why they remain in place

approaching three years
infinite room for both
your physical things
your spirit presence
in my heart of hearts
keeping your things
does no harm
no blame
poquito energy of your things
energy memories of golden times
comforts my embodied soul

October 8, 2014

# Looking Back

nearing third year anniversary
of your disembodiment
look back more often
remembering
reminiscing
than looking forward
looking back
counting my blessings
past present future
counting my losses
past present future
know need to make space
for your spirit presence
making slow progress
infinite room in my heart of hearts
looking back
indulging in reminisces
experiencing energy of memories
energy of love
approaching Disembodiment Day
Year Three
indulging in looking back
blessed with wonderful loving memories
share looking back
with your spirit presence

sometimes looking back
indulge in counting
my regrets for
errors of omission
errors of commission
squandering time

know I did OK
most of the time
looking back
hold myself to higher standard
explore each flaw blemish
fault shortcoming
know I did OK
most of the time
could have done better
perhaps burning and burning
in hellfires of grief
critical analysis of my flaws
pathway to compassion
authentic forgiveness
for my limitations
way to healing
you told me heart to heart
"forgiveness is the biggest
part of it"
your loving spirit presence
encouraging me to
count my blessings
forgive myself for my limitations
indulge myself in compassion
indulge myself in forgiveness
making slow progress
as we approach
Disembodiment Day Year Three
looking back
counting my blessings

October 13, 2014

Note: *Looking Back Looking Beyond* **Hellfires I**,
April 29, 2013, page 319

# Black Year Four

first year
wore black
only black

second year
wore black
added purple
now and then
mostly black

third year
wore black
added purple
now and then
mostly black
two colors' vibrations
match mine

fourth year
wear mostly black
with purple added
now and then
or
add colors
most likely wear black
with purple added
now and then
two colors' vibrations
match mine

October 17, 2014

# Healing Energy

not sure what healing looks like
know what healing feels like
experience healing energy
golden dreams
your spirit presence
golden hands holding our hearts together
our golden cocoon
I thought damaged beyond repair
slowly very slowly
converting black dragon named grief
into golden rainbow dragon
pair of golden rainbow dragons
infinite family of golden rainbow dragons
golden rainbow dragons been here all along
almost invisible looking with eyes of loss
golden rainbow energy
healing energy
transforming eyes of loss   grief vision
into
eyes of love   spirit vision
from eyes of love healing looks like
golden energy of eternal love
realize know what healing looks like
experience many forms
feel healing energy
energy of love eternal
pair of golden rainbow dragons
infinite family of golden rainbow dragons
healing energy of love
eternal love
thank you

October 19, 2014

# Laboratory of Alchemy

enter laboratory of alchemy via loss
larger the loss
larger the fire
hotter the fire
longer the burning
loss of loved one
biggest hottest longest fire
enter alchemical laboratory
even if use other names
grief mourning bereavement
admission automatic
with loss of loved one
alchemical fire
hellfires of grief
black invisible fire
burns without burning
hot without heat
focus on regrets remorse
errors of omission
errors of commission
sitting in alchemical crucible
burning and burning
ashes from burning
dissolved in water
tears of grief
hearts' tears
embodied soul's tears
black tears of grief
fire and water
separates gold from lead
realize essences

soul level awareness
may become more aware of
spirit realm
spirit level awareness
quintessence
eternal love
and beyond
alchemy of love
alchemy of loss
alchemy of grief
cycles of burning
hellfires of grief
cycles of tears of grief
soul's tears
slow   very slow transformation
alchemical transformation
vessel heart of hearts
alchemy of the heart
with good fortune
golden dreams
visits with loved one
in shared spirit realm home
spirit presence of loved one
provides improved awareness
soul vision
heart of hearts vision
transforms to
spirit vision
into spirit realm
and
experience of
eternal love

October 19, 2014

# Disembodiment Day: Year Three

three years ago today
your beautiful radiant spirit
left your physical body
returned to our spirit realm home
worst day of my life
followed by three years of
hellfires of grief
black nights of the soul
hard three years
black three years
missing your loving physical presence
longing for your return
grieving my loss our loss
black tears
seeing from eyes of
black dragon named grief
eyes of loss   grief vision
hard three years
black three years
black dragon within
drops lower towards
center of grief
heart of grief
heart of my heart
as I drop lower within
black dragon named grief
towards center of grief
heart of grief
heart of my heart

realize black dragon named grief
named Carlos Eldon
just like me
not our true name
good enough for now

surrounding Carlos Eldon the small
and black dragon of grief
named Carlos Eldon
golden rainbow dragons
golden rainbow dragon-fish
wonderful images
golden rainbow energy beings
ancestors and others
two closest in healing cocoon
Carol Susan my beloved
Carlos Eldon the large
I call the old alchemist
not their true names
good enough for now
names become unnecessary
words become unnecessary
images seen with
eyes of love
embodied soul's vision
spirit vision
within healing golden cocoon
black dragon named grief
slowly being assimilated
while I am
slowly being assimilated by
black dragon named grief
neither will ever be the same
no longer caterpillar

not yet butterfly
within chrysalis
golden rainbow cocoon
unsure we will emerge
on this side
or the other
or both
perhaps sinking lower into
heart of grief
will truly understand
no sides
coexist
now and then
looking at
black dragon named grief
with eyes of love
see black dragon has
golden rainbow aura
perhaps sinking lower into
heart of grief
will truly understand
heart of grief
heart of my heart
golden rainbow heart home of love

three hard years
three black years
at first could not see
golden rainbow cocoon
then blessed with golden dreams
visits to spirit realm
with by beloved Carol Susan
Carlos Eldon  ancestors  others
blessed with spirit presences

Carol Susan   Carlos Eldon
ancestors   others
whispers   inspirations
embodied soul's vision
transforming into
spirit vision

three hard years
three black years
now some times see
beyond black
golden rainbow cocoons
surrounded by
golden rainbow energy beings
eyes of loss   grief vision
coexisting with
eyes of love   spirit vision
blessings beyond measure
always forever and beyond
eternal love
thank you

Disembodiment Day Year Three
October 31, 2014

# Hellfires of Grief III

"...the fire has to burn the fire, one just has to burn in the emotion till the fire dies down and becomes balanced...the burning of the fire...has to be endured...the fire has to burn until the last unclean element had been consumed...suffered till what is mortal or corruptible...has been burned up...sitting in Hell and roasting there..."
Marie-Louise von Franz

hellfires of grief burn on and on
no end to love
no end to loss
no end to grief
while embodied
little less raw
little less heavy
little less dark
sometimes think I am
slowly climbing out of hellfires of grief
or perhaps just getting accustomed
to the flames
then dark images
dark memories
special days
hellfires of grief burn on and on
sitting in the flames
perhaps becoming more accustomed
to the fire
perhaps fewer impurities to burn
less fuel for the fire
increased compassion
increased forgiveness
for my human frailties
my beloved Carol Susan
whispered heart to heart

"it is mostly about forgiveness"
grieving for the loss of my beloved
struggling with my regrets remorse for
errors of omission
errors of commission
my human frailties
not my higher self Carlos Eldon
not the one I call the old alchemist
it is Carlos Eldon the small
the one roasting in the
hellfires of grief
accompanied by
black dragon named grief
also named Carlos Eldon
black dragon
may be bit smaller
hellfires may be bit smaller
or perhaps I am just
becoming more accustomed
to the flames
have made progress
more compassion
more forgiveness
after disembodiment of my beloved
at first experienced only black
hellfires of grief
burning and burning
focus only on loss
then golden dreams
my beloved's golden spirit presence
vision expanded
golden rainbow dragons
golden rainbow energy beings
Carol Susan   Carlos Eldon

ancestors   others
healing energy of spirit realm love

still sitting in hellfires of grief
burning and burning
now have other experiences
other memories
golden dreams
presence of my beloved
her soft whispers
surrounded by
golden rainbow energy beings
their golden hands
holding my broken hearts together
helping me heal
do not know how long
hellfires of grief
will last
now know how to transcend
hellfires of grief
visits to spirit realm
access spirit realm
transcendence only temporary
for now
return to hellfires of grief
perhaps not becoming
more accustomed to the flames
suspect golden rainbow energy
golden rainbow love
diminishes energy of
hellfires of grief
continue to experience
loss of my embodied soulmate
burning and burning

in hellfires of grief
also experience
golden rainbow
spirit realm love
blessed with
eternal love
thank you

October 23, 2014

Note: *Hellfires of Grief*, **Hellfires I**, January 1, 2012, page 68
*Hellfires of Grief II*, **Hellfires I,** April 25, 2013, page 336

Marie-Louise von Franz quote from:
Marie-Louise von Franz. Alchemy: **An Introduction to the Symbolism and the Psychology. Toronto:** Inner City Books, 1980, page 252.

Carol Susan

# Carol Susan 2014

### 1977

numinous power of the Feminine
natural expression of mysterious Yin ways
primal archetypal image of Woman
essence of flowering lotus
enchanting mythological princess
beautiful daughter of Tara
transformation's Divine Vessel
from you I see my changing
you guide by being you

you are also changing
we are becoming friends

### 2013

soulmates
spiritmates
always forever and beyond

### 2014

soulmatespiritmates
eternal love

C. Eldon Taylor
March 27, 2014

March 27, 1977-March 27, 2014
37 years

# Acknowledgements

**Celestial Helpers-Healers:**
Carol Susan, Carlos Eldon, and others

**Embodied Helpers-Healers:**
Carol Susan, Carlos Eldon, Taryne Jade, Denise Conner, Maya and Merlin, Lauren, Deb Cannon, Dede Dancing, Alice Claussen, Johanna Moorman, Carol Pollock, Nancy Powell, Julia Buchkina, and others

**Taylor DeVaney Wong Family Support**:
Especially Taryne Jade, Bob, Martha, Itzel, Manuella, Mater, Doris, Diana, Carmen, Alfonso, Fanny and Tommy, Ceci, Chicho, and others

# Selected References

Avila, Elena. **Woman Who Glows in the Dark: A Curandera Reveals Traditional Aztec Secrets of Physical and Spiritual Health.** New York: Tracher/Penguin, 1999.

Boa, Fraser. **The Way of the Dream: Conversations on Jungian Dream Interpretation with Marie-Louise von Franz.** Boston: Shambhala, 1994.

Brennan, Barbara Ann. **Light Emerging: The Journey of Personal Healing.** New York: Bantam Books, 1993.

Brennan, Barbara Ann. **Hands of Light: A Guide to Healing Through the Human Energy Field.** New York: Bantam Books, 1988.

Castaneda, Carlos. **Journey to Ixtlan: The Lessons of Don Juan.** New York: Simon and Schuster, 1972.

Fortune, Dion. **Through the Gates of Death** (1930) republished as **Dion Fortune's Book of the Dead.** Boston: Weiser Books, 2005.

Fox, John. **Poetic Medicine: The Healing Art of Poem-Making.** New York: Jeremy P. Tarcher, 1997.

George, Demetra. **Mysteries of the Dark Moon: The Healing Power of the Dark Goddess.** New York: HarperCollins, 1992.

Halifax, Joan. **Being with Dying: Cultivating Compassion and Fearlessness in the Presence of Death.** Boston: Shambhala, 2009.

Halifax, Joan. **The Fruitful Darkness: Reconnecting with the Body of the Earth.** San Francisco: HarperCollins, 1993.

Hall, Donald. **The Best Day The Worst Day: Life with Jane Kenyon: A Memoir.** Boston: Houghton Mifflin Company, 2005.

Hall, Donald. **Without: Poems.** Boston: Houghton Mifflin Company, 1998.

Hillman, James and Shamdasani, Sonu. **Lament of the Dead: Psychology after Jung's Red Book.** New York: W.W. Norton & Co., 2013.

Hillman, James. **The Dream and the Underworld.** New York: Harper & Row, Publishers, 1997.

Kubler-Ross, Elizabeth and Kessler, David. **On Grief and Grieving: Finding the Meaning of Grief Through the Five Stages of Loss.** New York: Scribner, 2005.

Moore, Thomas. **Dark Nights of the Soul: A Guide to Finding Your Way Through Life's Ordeals.** New York: Penguin, 2004.

Moore, Thomas. **The Reinchantment of Everyday Life.** New York: HarperCollins, 1996.

Moore, Thomas. **Soul Mates: Honoring the Mysteries of Love and Relationship.** New York: HarperCollins, 1994.

Scully, Nicki. **Alchemical Healing: A Guide To Spiritual, Physical, and Transformational Medicine.** Rochester, Vermont: Bear & Company, 2003.

Sterling, Peter. **Harp Magic.** Sedona, Arizona: Harp Magic Music, 1993/2004.

Sullins, Angi and Toball, Silas. **A Knock at the Door.** Portland, Oregon: Amber Lotus Publishing, 2008.

Taylor, Jeremy. **The Wisdom of Your Dreams: Using Dreams To Tap Into Your Unconscious and Transform Your Life.** New York: Jeremy P. Tarcher, 2009.

Villoldo, Alberto. **Courageous Dreaming: How Shamans Dream the World Into Being.** Carlsbad, California: Hay House, 2008.

Villoldo, Alberto. **Shaman, Healer, Sage: How To Heal Yourself and Others with the Energy Medicine of the Americas.** New York: Harmony Books, 2000.

Virtue, Doreen. **Healing with the Angels: How the Angels Can Assist You in Every Area of Your Life.** Carlsbad, California: Hay House, 1999.

von Franz, Marie-Louise. **On Dreams & Death.** Boston: Shambhala, 1987.

von Franz, Marie-Louise. **Alchemy: An Introduction to the Symbolism and the Psychology.** Toronto: Inner City Books, 1980.

Wei, Wu. **I Ching Wisdom: Volume One: Guidance from the Book of Changes.** Los Angeles: Power Press, 2005.

Wilhelm, Richard (translator) Baynes, Cary F. (English translation). **The I Ching or Book of Changes, Volume I.** London: Routledge and Kegan Paul, Ltd., 1951.

Wong, Eva (translator). **Harmonizing Yin and Yang: The Dragon-Tiger Classic.** Boston: Shambhala, 1997.

Yalom, Irvin D. **Staring At The Sun: Overcoming the Terror of Death.** San Francisco: Jossey-Bass, 2009.

# Author

**C. Eldon Taylor** is a psychotherapist licensed as a Licensed Professional Counselor (LPC-Virginia), Licensed Mental Health Counselor (LMHC-Florida), and National Certified Counselor. None of which was much help when it became his turn to experience the hellfires of grief and dark nights of the soul after the disembodiment of his beloved Carol Susan.

Eldon is currently writing **Golden Dreams II: Companion to Hellfires of Grief II: More Love Poems** which will be published in 2015. The **Hellfires I** and **Hellfires II** books describe my daytime experience of the first three years of bereavement in 444 poems. **Golden Dreams I** and **Golden Dreams II** describe the dreamtime experience for the same three year time period (plus a bit) in 222 dreams converted into poems.

Eldon is also writing **Alchemy of the Heart: Love Loss Grief Transformation Eternal Love** which will be published in 2015. **Alchemy of the Heart** uses the first four books of poems as raw material to develop a description of love, loss, grief, and transformation to eternal love using images and processes of alchemy. Part I: theoretical alchemy converts the images in the four books of poems into a description of the processes experienced burning in the hellfires of grief. Part II: applied laboratory alchemy provides 111 "things that helped" the process of transformation with the laboratory being three years of bereavement. **Alchemy of the Heart** is the distilled essence of the four books of poems. The five books together provide both the raw material for the work of alchemy of the heart and the results to date of the alchemical journey into the black nights of the soul and beyond.

**Contact Information:
celdontaylor@gmail.com**

# Other Books

**Hellfires of Grief: Love Poems.** C. Eldon Taylor (2012)

222 poems covering first 18 months of bereavement

**Golden Dreams: Companion to Hellfires of Grief: Love Poems.** Carlos Eldon Taylor and Carol Susan DeVaney-Wong (2013)

111 dream poems covering first 18 months of bereavement

**Golden Dreams II: Companion to Hellfires of Grief II: More Love Poems.** Carlos Eldon Taylor and Carol Susan DeVaney-Wong (in process, expected publication date 2015)

111 dream poems covering second 18 months plus of bereavement

**Alchemy of the Heart: Love Loss Grief Transformation Eternal Love.** C. Eldon Taylor (in process, expected publication date 2015)

**Part I:** Theoretical Alchemy. Images and processes of alchemy applied to loss, grief and transformation
**Part II:** Laboratory Alchemy. Transformation with the laboratory being the hellfires of grief (practical application: what helps)

www.ingramcontent.com/pod-product-compliance
Lightning Source LLC
Chambersburg PA
CBHW032058090426
42743CB00007B/159